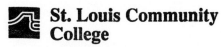

St. Louis Community College

Forest Park
Florissant Valley
Meramec

Instructional Resources
St. Louis, Missouri

CHILD CARE
A PARENT'S GUIDE
SECOND EDITION

Sonja Cooper

™ Facts On File, Inc.

CHILD CARE: A PARENT'S GUIDE, Second Edition

Copyright © 1991, 1999 by Sonja Cooper
First edition 1991
Second edition 1999

Checkmark Books
An imprint of Facts On File
11 Penn Plaza
New York, NY 10001

Library of Congress Cataloging-in-Publication Data

Cooper, Sonja.
    Child care : a parent's guide / Sonja Cooper. — 2nd ed.
      p. cm.
    Includes bibliographical references and index.
    ISBN 0-8160-3858-9 (hc. : alk paper). — ISBN 0-8160-3859-7
(pbk. : alk. paper)
    1. Child care—United States. 2. Child care services—United
States. I. Title.
    HQ778.63.C64 1999
    362.71'2'0973—dc21   98–38361

Checkmark Books are available at special discounts when purchased in bulk
quantities for businesses, associations, institutions or sales promotions.
Please call our Special Sales Department in New York at (212) 967-8800
or (800) 322-8755.

You can find Facts On File on the World Wide Web at http://www.factsonfile.com

Text design by Donna Sinisgalli
Cover design by Maria Ilardi

Printed in the United States of America

MP FOF 10 9 8 7 6 5 4 3 2 1
    (pbk) 10 9 8 7 6 5 4 3 2 1

This book is printed on acid-free paper.

Contents

Acknowledgments

I'd like to thank the many parents, educators and other professionals who shared their experiences and expertise with me. Special thanks go to Child Action, Inc., Sacramento, California, for its guidelines in choosing quality child care and to Work/Family Directions. Please refer to the resource section for more information about these and other valuable groups.

I greatly appreciate my family, including my parents, Dr. Armin Bickel and Erna Bickel, my brother Tom Bickel and his wife Lina and children Thomas, Jessica and Amy. Special thanks to my sister, Heidi Jewell, for her support, strength and love during a very difficult year (it's your turn to shine). I can't think of my family without a remembrance to my big brother, Pete Bickel. The memory of your smile warms my heart.

My survival partner, Janet Steinbach, is still my soul sister and always will be. We've gone through so much together: marriage, childbirth, divorce. I can't imagine life without our friendship.

To Laughter Works Seminars for teaching me how to laugh again. And to Jim Pelley, my soul mate, who taught me how to embrace risk, manage change and keep the door to love wide open.

Lastly, to my daughter, Lyndsay Flatting. I've watched you grow into such a beautiful young woman. You are strong, resilient and incredibly gifted in so many ways. I thank God for you and your sense of humor. I would want to be your pal even if we weren't related. You're one in a million, kid. I love you.

My Introduction to Child Care

When I was pregnant with my daughter, I met an apparently mature teenager who claimed to have extensive experience with babies—especially newborns—and who was thrilled at the prospect of a new charge. Since my husband and I had decided that I would stay at home with the baby for the first few years, I felt that having one name and telephone number would be enough for those times we wanted to get away for a few hours. Besides, we were going to expose our child to the world by taking her to restaurants and on outings with us. We'd still have lots of time together as a couple when she slept. (I'd heard babies did that a lot.) Things were well under control.

One week after Lyndsay Dawn Flating came into the world we were put to the test when an important corporate dinner made an appearance necessary. After reviewing six pages of copious notes with the babysitter, we strode confidently into the night air for our first time away from the baby. This was going to be easy!

That seems like such a long time ago. The evening ended in tears for both mom and baby after the sitter gave my six-day-old baby refrigerated apple juice! I had a lot of time that night to think about child care as Lyndsay screamed until dawn. I decided it wasn't worth the risk; no one could take care of her the way I did. And no one did—until it became clear after several months that my sanity was hanging by a very thin thread.

It was simply too complicated to take the baby along on most errands when my own stamina and postpartum depression made even the simplest tasks overwhelming. Although well-read on pregnancy and childbirth, I was totally unprepared for the demanding schedule of a newborn. If I managed to shower and get out of my robe by the time my husband came home from work, I considered the day a success. Unfortunately, my husband was little help. He was a first-time father at the age of 36, and in spite of the prebaby rhetoric, he continued his work and tennis schedule without interruption. He had originally planned to be home with me for the first week to help out. But by noon of my first day home from the hospital, the office was on the phone, and he was out the door.

"You can handle it, can't you honey?" he asked.

I remember the hurt and disappointment. We both dismissed my tears as merely hormonal. After all, I was Superwoman.

Obviously, not everyone has severe postpartum depression. But because of a lack of support, physical exhaustion and isolation, I was ready to run away—until I finally got rid of my Superwoman cape. After a very long time and a lot of Kleenex, I was able to get some perspective on the situation and develop a plan to deal with things on a different level.

One of the first things I did was arrange for child care on a regular basis so I could get out of the house! By now, Lyndsay was three months old. This time I ran an ad in the newspaper and received a handful of responses. I hired the one and only woman who came to the house for an interview. Linda was in her mid-thirties but had no experience with children. Still, she seemed so nice, and I liked the way Lyndsay disappeard in the folds of her massive arms. I didn't call any of her references because I didn't know what to ask them beyond, "What do you think of Linda?" Besides, people only list references that they know will say nice things about them, so why bother, I thought.

When Lyndsay finally began sleeping through the night and Linda started coming two afternoons a week, life began to get back to normal. It was wonderful to play tennis again, grocery shop with ease or just take a nap, knowing Lyndsay was in good hands.

About three weeks after Linda started caring for Lyndsay, my husband and I called her on a Sunday to see if she would watch the baby while we played mixed doubles for two hours. Linda was there within the hour, and we left for the tennis court.

But something didn't feel right. I couldn't keep my mind on the tennis match and felt anxious about being away from home. We turned down an invitation for dinner and went right home instead. Ironically, the conversation on the way home revolved around how our lives had changed for the better since Linda had started working for us. Just between the two of us, we felt smug about having solved our child care dilemma with relative ease.

I was the first one through the door and sensed something terribly wrong even before I saw anything. My memories from that point on are all in slow motion.

Lyndsay was dangling in mid-air as Linda held her by only one foot! Lyndsay's arms were thrashing, but no sound came out of my baby's throat. She was alternately purple, then blue. Linda began babbling something about the baby spitting up and choking. Lyndsay managed to make strangling sounds every minute or so, only to stop, turn blue and go limp again.

Ken and I panicked. We now know we should have dialed 911 for emergency help (they have oxygen on the trucks), but all we could think of was to get Lyndsay to a hospital.

After what seemed like hours, we reached the emergency room. I was out of the car before it came to a full stop and ran inside, carrying my now-limp baby. The hospital personnel didn't bother with formalities—a nurse grabbed her out of my arms and disappeared down the hall. Minutes later, more people ran in the same direction. By the time I caught up with them, they had a tracheotomy kit ready. They were going to cut my baby's throat unless she started breathing on her own.

Four hours later we took Lyndsay home with careful instructions from the hospital. The phone was ringing as we walked through the door; it was Linda. She had been worried sick about Lyndsay and had been trying to reach us all night. That's when I got the whole story.

Linda had been changing Lyndsay's diaper when Lyndsay started to spit up her apple juice (apple juice, again!). Instead of flipping Lyndsay over onto her stomach, Linda put her hand over Lyndsay's mouth to keep her from making a mess. By the time Linda picked her up to burp her, Lyndsay was already choking. Linda didn't know what to do, so she tried shaking her upside down, with no results. That's when we walked through the door.

Linda never came back to our house again. In fact, we stopped using child care altogether. I'd learned my lesson. I should have checked Linda's references, interviewed more people before making a selection and gone over my expectations in detail with Linda. Linda wasn't guilty of neglect, just ignorance. I was the one who should have played "what if" with her during the interview instead of winging it with questions made up on the spot. I should have spent time with Linda and Lyndsay before leaving them alone together, I should have insisted on a CPR course . . . I should have . . . I should have . . . There are so many things I should have done to prevent this near-tragedy. If it meant giving up tennis, friends and romance, I was never going to leave my child in unsafe hands again—and I didn't until a year later when my husband started a family business.

The thought of using child care filled me with dread. I dreaded the hassle, the uncertainty and the danger. To add to my stress, I did not want to work full time while my baby was still young but felt I had very little choice. Would my fears affect the success of my search?

I began by calling a resource and referral agency listed under "Child Care" in the yellow pages. They were very helpful in providing names and telephone numbers of licensed homes and centers in my area, but I needed more than that. I needed to know what was right for me *before checking out the options,* and that meant homework. I had so many questions. How could I avoid making the wrong choice again?

Are there any magic questions to ask that reveal more than others? I wondered. How could I feel more in control of the situation when my knees literally shook every time I thought about leaving my child in the hands of a stranger? Do good parents use child care?

I needed a system of gathering information and guidelines for evaluating that information. Only then could I make an informed decision about the best type of care for *my* child at that particular point in our lives. I also knew that no matter how good her care was, I would have to be sold on it if it was going to work.

This book is a result of my quest. By learning about all types of child care options, including nontraditional ideas, and examing the emotional side of child care, I sincerely believe that *anyone* can solve their child care dilemma. There is an ideal provider out there—all you have to do is eliminate the barriers that keep you from finding that person. And you've just taken the first step!

It is my hope that this book will save you time, effort and frustration in your own child care search, so I'll begin by answering the most important question first: Yes, good parents do use child care.

1

EARLY MEMORIES OF CHILD CARE

I was born in the fifties, raised in the sixties and married in the seventies. Child care went through a lot of changes during those years. My earliest memory of child care was the hushed tones my mom used with the neighbors when discussing "poor Freddy down the street" whose mother (gasp!) worked full-time—and she didn't even have to! We all looked at Freddy slightly askance, waiting for a mass murderer to emerge. It was understood that Freddy was saved only through the nurturance provided by my mother until his came home from work (a bargain at about $2 a day). What kind of a woman would leave her child in someone else's care? The kindest thing I remember hearing about Freddy's mom was that she was selfish.

Obviously, my small world was out of sync with the reality presented every day on TV. Everyone was so happy at home.

One of the first clues to the possibility of domestic disharmony came on—of all shows—*Father Knows Best*. It was the first time I saw a glimmer of normalcy on TV.

The show opened with the mother, Jane, up to her elbows in dirty dishes, children all around making demands and a hurried husband trying to get out the door but unable to find his briefcase (even then I wondered why the mother had to keep track of everything). After the family was gone, Jane tried to pump herself up to tackle the day's laundry, dishes, shopping, meal planning, volunteer work, sewing and baking with a sunny smile and a twinkle in her eye. So far, very predictable. Then a far-off look replaced the twinkle for just a second before she dove back into her work. But what's this? She pauses a second time. By now she's got my full attention. Here was a Mom who didn't act like a Mom.

The story lines takes Jane out of the kitchen for a day of self-indulgence. She drives herself to an unfamiliar part of town and spontaneously has her portrait painted by a street artist. Suddenly she sees a familiar face and bolts back to the safety of her home before she is recognized. Don't ask me how, but the artist tracks her down and delivers the portrait to her home—in front of the whole family. Mom clearly has a lot of explaining to do to her stunned family. Not only that, but the house is still a wreck and it is past dinner time! Stammering and stuttering, Jane explains that she doesn't know what got into her, but she just had to get out of the house and do something for herself—just once. She's sorry, it will never happen again. Kindly, Jim embraces her like the forgiving father that he is and dismisses the whole thing as a lark not to be taken seriously. He'll just forget it ever happened.

I sat wide-eyed at the end of the show with some very serious questions buzzing around my juvenile brain. In the first place, I didn't think moms ever had feelings like real people—they were towers of strength who never got sick or sad or restless. At the same time, what was so hard to understand? I thought Jane had every right to take a day off without having to justify it to her family. I lost respect for her because she was so passive about her needs, and yet, that's what moms did, didn't they?

I was glad my mom was one of the "good" mothers who stayed home with her children and (bonus points) actually took care of someone else's child in the process, an observation I took great pains to reinforce to Freddy at every opportunity. It was with great pride that I was unable to relate to having a babysitter—ever.

It's no wonder I had such trouble leaving my own child!

By the time my mother went to work, my siblings and I were all in school and old enough to take care of ourselves until she got home each day. But it wasn't the same. The house was always a little emptier and colder when she wasn't there. There were still no role models on TV for working mothers, but more and more of my friends' moms were out there in the workplace. It became inevitable that the days of warm cookies and milk were over for us. We were selfish children, used to having our mother make our beds and clean our messes.

There were some shows that portrayed atypical families—*The Courtship of Eddie's Father*, *Bachelor Father*, and *Family Affair*—but no single mothers (Kate and Allie, where were you?).

I mention old TV shows because they had such an impact on me. Everything I knew about society came from that small box. Because my parents immigrated from Germany when I was five years old and they struggled with culture clash on a daily basis, they too relied on TV to provide role models.

The message was very clear: Good mothers stayed home and lived their lives through their families. They were walking resources for anyone who needed anything.

Most single career women on TV at that time were portrayed as desperate or ditsy (remember Sally on the *Dick Van Dyke Show?*).

It was not until the seventies that my views changed about a woman's role in society or, specifically, about my role in society. I moved through a teenage feminist period filled with righteous anger because it was fashionable at first and later because I had gathered enough life experience under my belt to understand where that anger came from. Child care was still not considered something good mothers did (dads never got mentioned), but it was conceivable that certain mothers had to work, either because of economics or because of a special talent that could not be denied.

For some reason, it was okay in my community to put your child in the church nursery during regular meetings of the women's club but not okay to enroll her in a private nursery school. Clearly, the child care issue was one loaded with controversy.

A course on women's history answered many of the questions with which I struggled during those years as well as raising a few new ones. For instance, we discussed how during World War II women were expected to work in defense plants while their children were being cared for in private or federally-funded child care centers. Edgar F. Kaiser established two child care centers at his shipyards with federal support. These centers provided 24-hour-a-day, seven-day-a-week service for the children of his 28,500 women workers. Needless to say, the demand far exceeded the supply. Companies laid off the women to make room for the returning men. They also initiated policies making it impossible for spouses to work together. Since there was such a shortage of jobs available, the women usually gave up theirs. The government began a campaign to glamourize staying home (compare pre- and postwar ads).

The course taught me several basic principles about the history of child care: It's a long stretch between Donna Reed and Rosie the Riveter; society can be fickle; child care is a political as well as emotional issue; and finally, the need for quality child care that is both affordable and accessible has been around for a long, long time.

Perhaps the first place to begin when discussing child care is to look at our own biases toward the subject. Obviously, the way we were raised has a lot to do with the way we want to raise our own children. Because I never experienced any form of child care when I was growing up, I had a tough time coming to terms with my own need for a child care provider. I didn't understand the source of my anxiety until developing the Self Test. This helped me realize why the thought of child care filled me with anxiety, guilt and a feeling of failure.

It's time to air out all those preconceived ideas.

The Self Test: Narrowing the Focus

Each family is unique in its child care needs and expectations. How do you arrive at a decision about what's right for your family without going through the disruption and danger of trial and error?

The answer lies in exploring all aspects of child care *before* you pick up the phone to follow your first lead. Once you have a clear idea of your needs and expectations, the rest is a matter of research. *The toughest part is getting started.*

The Self Test is designed to narrow your focus by eliminating certain child care choices and concentrating on the method most likely to work for your family. There will still be a trial and error period with any method of child care, but your chances for success are far greater if you do your homework first. It's important to stress that **no one is able to take your place—your goal is to find someone who will do a good job in your absence.**

Some questions are designed to bring out hidden fears and expectations while other questions deal with the nuts and bolts of finance and time commitment. Why not share the test with other family members and compare answers? The results may surprise you!

Directions: Answer the following questions on a separate sheet of paper. The end result will be a statement of needs for you to use as the foundation for your child care search (see sample). After you have finished the Self Test, put it away for a day or two before you review the answers again. Revise and rewrite your statement of needs until it sounds right. This is the first and most important step in solving your child care dilemma, so take time to answer the questions completely.

1. The perfect environment for my child is:
2. I prefer to have my child's care take place:
   - a. in my home
   - b. in someone else's home
   - c. in a center-based facility
   - d. no preference
3. I would like my child:
   - a. to be exposed to other children his/her own age
   - b. to be exposed to other children a variety of ages
   - c. to have one-on-one care with no other children around
4. I need before and/or after school care for my child near:
   - a. my home
   - b. my work place
   - c. my child's school
5. I also need transportation for my child to and/or from school:
   yes or no

---

6. The worst situation for my child would be:
7. The perfect situation would be:
   (Include characteristics you would like the provider to have, such as creativity, humor, patience, commitment to good nutrition, special training, etc.) If your perfect situation involves a group environment, describe the ages of other children and a physical description (large home with a backyard full of safe play equipment, a child care center with no more than 50 children, etc.).
8. What would happen on a "worst case" basis if I used child care regularly? (examples: warped personality, transfer of affection to the provider)
9. What is the best thing that would happen if I used child care on a regular basis?
10. I've been putting off finding child care because:
    a. I don't want to do it
    b. lack of money
    c. lack of knowledge about what's available and how to locate information
    d. laziness—it's too much work
    e. other :
11. Which best describes the time commitment I need from a caregiver?
    a. open-ended—This is still an experiment. I just want a list of people I can call when and if I need someone.
    b. part-time—days and hours flexible, but a definite number of hours per week
    c. part-time permanent—same days and hours each week
    d. full-time permanent—I want the caregiver to be a part of the family.
    e. live-in—room and board in exchange for child care (with or without salary)
    f. other :
12. Which other important qualities should my provider have?
13. What are intolerable traits (such as, smoking) or situations (including their own children while caring for mine)?
14. If light housework is to be included, list specific jobs and how often they will need to be done (vacuuming every other day, beds made daily, dishes done daily, dusting, etc.).
15. Describe an ideal typical day between my child and the caregiver.
16. What is my policy on discipline? Toilet training? Number of hours the TV is on during the day?
17. What is my monthly budget for child care? Am I willing to exchange child care hours with another mother?

18. What is my backup plan on those days when the caregiver is ill or unavailable?
19. How soon do I need someone?
20. Am I ready to make a decision about child care?

The last question is important because although you may have a tremendous need for child care, unless you are psychologically ready to begin, your efforts may be wasted. But don't feel discouraged if you don't feel ready yet. That's why you're reading this book, remember? After we've gone through the process, step by step, you'll be ready, willing and able to tackle the child care dilemma. Don't be surprised if it turns out to be fun, too.

Sample Self Test

The following sample Self Test was taken with an eight-year-old child in mind. I've numbered the responses to correspond with the questions to demonstrate how the Self Test becomes your unique statement of needs.

[1] The perfect environment for my child is a home-like atmosphere in [2] someone else's home, since I work out of my own home. I would like my child to be [3] exposed to other children her own age. I need [4] after school care only for my child near her school. [5] I do not need transportation either to or from school.

[6] The worst situation would be one in which there were no other children and nothing for her to do until I picked her up. [7] The perfect situation would be a small family day care home with one other child her age and maybe an infant to play with. It would be run by a child-oriented, highly nurturing mother motivated by her love for children rather than her high profit margin. Her home would be safe with lots of outdoor activities in a fenced backyard. My child would have access to a telephone and permission to call me if needed. [8] If I use child care on a regular basis I would feel guilty and worry about long-range effects on the relationship between my child and me. [9] However, the best thing about using child care on a regular basis would be the opportunity for my child to develop social skills and relate to another adult—an adult whose day is structured around the needs of children. [10] I've been putting off finding child care because of laziness.

[11] I need someone on a part-time basis, same days and hours each week, with flexibility for extra hours as needed—possibly even evenings and an occasional weekend. This is negotiable. [12] That person should be stable, patient, loving, experienced (possibly with college credits in child development) and committed. [13] I will not tolerate smokers, big dogs, dark living rooms or prima donnas.

[15] A typical day would include after-school activities ranging from quiet times to active play, a healthy snack, time set aside for homework and one or two TV shows. [16] Time out (removal from an activity or the other children) is to be used for discipline, not to exceed 20 minutes maximum in the severest cases, followed by discussion. Under no circumstances will I tolerate any form of corporal punishment. [17] My monthly budget for part-time child care is $150. [18] I want the provider to be responsible for backup care in case of emergency. If backup care isn't available on a specific day, I'll rearrange my schedule. [19] I need a child care plan in effect by September 8th. [20] I'm not ready to do it yet, but I will be after I finish this book.

Now it's your turn. Your answers will serve as the blueprint for your search. Use a three-ring binder with pockets to store the results of the Self Test and to organize the wealth of information you will be gathering about child care.

2
MOTIVATION FOR FINDING CHILD CARE

We've all read horrible accounts in newspapers and magazines about child care providers whose neglect and/or abuse has resulted in tragedy.

- ❖ Three toddlers drowned in the swimming pool of an unlicensed day care center . . .
- ❖ Elizabeth was permanently blinded by the violent shaking an unlicensed nanny gave her . . .
- ❖ A day care director was charged with molesting five children . . .
- ❖ A family was charged with felony child endangerment after a 16-month-old girl apparently strangled to death on a leash at their unlicensed day care home . . .

Unfortunately, negative publicity often causes all day care providers to be perceived as guilty until proven innocent. It's no wonder parents are reluctant to begin the search for quality day care! Yet the need for child care is greater than ever.

People seek child care for a variety of reasons, including:

1. *Economic necessity.* This is especially true in view of the increase in the number of single parent households and the difficulty of making ends meet on only one paycheck in two-parent households.
2. *Socialization for the child.* Child care is an excellent way to expose your child to social situations in a child-oriented environment. Only children benefit from this type of exposure as well as children with siblings, especially if the siblings are far apart in age.
3. *Stress reduction for the parent.* Let's face it, the demands of parenthood frequently create the need for periods of "time out." Sometimes as little as two hours of child care a week can make a tremendous difference in the life of a stressed-out parent. A little rejuvenation goes a long way.

What Are Your Reasons for Seeking Child Care?

Because our priorities are all so different, what works in one family may be totally inappropriate for another. That's why it's important to keep an open mind but make the final decision based on your own gut feelings rather than the recommendation of friends or relatives. Regardless of the environment you eventually choose for your child, keep in mind that child care needs to address five basic needs of children:

- Physical needs—space and equipment
- Socialization skills—how to get along with other people
- Emotional needs—love and attention
- Preparation for the future—learning how to fit into the world
- Freedom to express the sheer joy of childhood—a safe, happy place to be a kid

With these needs in mind, lets take a look at the following situations, each with a unique demand and solution.

Remember: Your motivation will directly affect the success or failure of your search.

See if you recognize parts of yourself in the following pages.

Julia. A divorced mother of three children ages 10 years, eight years and 19 months, Julia is employed by the state because "it offers great benefits, decent hours and the chance for advancement for someone with a limited education." Julia married young and stayed home with her children until she became divorced. Child care is her number one concern.

Discussions with her co-workers didn't provide many answers because the majority of them either have grown children or relatives to provide child care. Julia had never really thought about what she wanted from child care beyond a situation that would work for all three children. Her salary plus child support payments make it impossible for her to budget more than $600 per month for child care, an amount she found to be inadequate even though the two older children are in school most of the day. She tried placing a notice on the bulletin board at the grocery store with disastrous results, including having to change her phone number to avoid a stranger who kept calling shortly after the ad was placed.

The yellow pages provided the phone number of a resource and referral service which was helpful in providing the names and phone numbers of licensed providers in her area but couldn't help her decide what was right for her. She didn't have the answers to many child care questions herself. Furthermore, she certainly couldn't take the time to visit each facility or even call for information during work hours. And by the time she got home at night, fed the kids, supervised homework and told bedtime stories, she was too exhausted to get on the phone to interview prospective family day care homes and felt uncomfortable about calling so late.

The baby was currently in an unlicensed home in her neighborhood because it was convenient and the woman charged less than a licensed home. The older children rode their bikes home after school and stayed indoors until Julia came home. She hated the thought of having latchkey children, but what else could she do? She also worried about the baby since there were so many other infants in the home—too many. This system was frail, at best, with too many interruptions at work in the afternoon. Julia's productivity went down dramatically between three and five o'clock when the kids came home to an empty house. She made and received numerous phone calls to check on the kids, settle disputes and answer homework questions. Even on those afternoons when the phone at her desk was relatively quiet, Julia worried about the effect this situation would have on her children, not to mention the physical problems she experienced on a daily basis caused by the stress.

When asked to describe her life, Julia answered: "Fear, anxiety, juggling, putting out fires, living one day—and sometimes one hour—at a time, overburdened and stressed." She was completely overwhelmed by the adjustments of being a single parent and could not imagine a time when she would have time for herself, let alone begin dating again. Her one fantasy was to be in a position to rebuild her life with the confidence that her children were not only being taken care of but were thriving in an environment of her choosing.

Nancy. A 39-year-old college professor and mother of a six-week-old baby boy, Nancy and her husband, Phil, a corporate attorney, were married for almost 20 years before their son was born. Nancy and her husband enjoyed an active social life with lots of travel during this time.

Now, six weeks after Adam's birth, a new fear has crept into Nancy's life along with a serious case of postpartum depression. She is beginning to wonder if she can do it all without sacrificing the things she and Phil have built their lives around. The baby wants to eat every two hours, sleeps lightly and sporadically and seems so demanding. Nancy was used to being in control at work as well as at home. Although they could easily afford child care, Nancy and Phil decided when they first found out she was pregnant that they would share the responsibilities of raising their child—not turn everything over to some stranger.

Phil had been the center of attention at every dinner party during her pregnancy due to his involved fatherhood philosophy. Men and women alike admired his attitude. Nancy only occasionally caught the looks several of the mothers in the group gave each other but passed them off as being caused by jealousy. Now she wasn't so sure—things were definitely not working out as planned.

Some days Nancy didn't even get dressed—why bother, with night and day running together the way they did? The house could have qualified for federal aid, and food consisted of take-out roulette. Lately Phil was spending more time at the office because of a heavy caseload, although in the past he had always brought his work home. He was great when the baby was clean, dry and full but disappeared at the sound of crying. Maybe this wasn't how he thought it would be, either. Who would blame him for not wanting to come home?

The worst part was not having anyone to talk to about her feelings. Everyone thought she would handle motherhood the same way she handled everything else—with cool reserve and professionalism. She felt her identity slipping into a very scary gray area.

Was it really just last year that little Adam was conceived in a four-star hotel on Maui?

Nancy hid her depression only when Phil brought home friends to see the new baby. Then she slipped into her Superwoman role and stifled the impulse to strangle Phil. How could things have gotten so far offtrack? There was no doubt in her mind that something was going to snap soon—either her sanity or her marriage, or both.

Matt. Middle manager for a lumber brokerage firm, 34 years old, widower with a six-year-old daughter, Monica, who developed a history of asthma after her mother's death—this describes Matt. Matt misses an average of three days of work each month because of Monica's frail health and is in serious danger of losing his place in the fast track because of these absences.

Although his company offers employee assistance with child care, Matt is apprehensive about going public with his problems. He continues to use his mother for child care because she is familiar with Monica's needs, even though it means he has to listen to a barrage of unwanted advice each time he returns from a business trip. Besides, he doesn't want Monica with "strangers" because no one can care for her like he can. He would really like to do something about his situation but sees no way out.

Like Nancy, Matt is having a hard time seeing the light at the end of the tunnel. He chooses to believe things will work out by themselves and sees no way to control the forces that pull at his life. When asked what his biggest concern is, Matt answers without hesitation, "My own health. Lately I get these migraines that incapacitate me to where I can't go to work or take care of Monica. I feel completely paralyzed at those times. And if something happens to me or my job, what will happen to my child?"

Janet and Bill. Janet and Bill are in their late twenties and have three-year-old twins. Bill is in the Air Force; Janet returned to work when the twins were six-weeks-old. Her sister has cared for them all this time. Bill has just been transferred, and since he and Janet are new to the area, they have no idea where to begin looking for child care help. Janet and Bill both believe it would be a good idea for the twins to be around other children their own age but are concerned about all the bad publicity surrounding day care in general.

Janet loves children and has been considering the idea of staying home for a while, but she needs new challenges in her life to be happy. Both parents are actively involved in the daily nurturing and care of their children. They have a beautiful home with a large yard full of play equipment, trees, bike trails and a bunny hutch (a new addition to the family with the hopes it will ease the transition to a new town). Except for the six weeks following the birth of her children, Janet has always worked, and they have come to depend on two incomes. Now that the boxes are unpacked, Janet is faced with a dilemma.

Cynthia and Chuck. This couple has waited years for their baby. Cynthia's job will still be there after her three-month maternity leave, and Chuck is genuinely enthusiastic. He has even taken baby care classes on his own so he will be better able to care for his child. Cynthia's mother is ecstatic about caring for her grandchild after Cynthia returns to work and has already "baby-proofed" her home in anticipation. Everything is in place except the baby. So why does Cynthia have such a knot in her stomach?

Dana. She never thought she would become a statistic. After being married for 10 years, Dana and Ben decided the best course of action was separate lives.

It was very difficult for Robby, their nine-year-old son. His way of coping was to misbehave in school by bullying younger kids, disrupting class, swearing and refusing to obey his mother. Robby had had excellent before- and after-school care at his elementary school, but because of his violent outbursts and for the safety of the group, Dana had been told to find other arrangements. She was absolutely heartbroken over her child's pain as well as her own. On a good day, she coped. On a bad day, she lost her temper, hit Robby and spent the rest of the evening feeling guilty.

Ben was very little help; he became a "Disneyland Dad" on weekends to compensate for not being there during the week and felt too guilty to discipline Robby when Robby got out of line. After all, Ben saw him so seldom that he didn't want to alienate him. It took two days to get things back to normal after a weekend with his dad—two very long, trying days. Dana felt a male role model was important for Robby but didn't know anyone who would invest the time and attention. Unaware of the many community agencies available, Dana decided against counseling due to finances. So the cycle continued: anger, pain, guilt and helplessness/hopelessness.

"Had I stayed married, I would have been unhappy, but nothing could be worse than this," she said. "At least I wouldn't have to worry about money or a job, and Robby would have a real family."

Dana seriously considered going back to Ben to ease her financial and emotional burden. It was either that or continue the struggle for years to come—if she lived that long.

In a Nutshell

Motivation takes many forms. The preceding six examples are based on the following situations.

1. In your heart of hearts, you do not want to be away from your children and deeply resent being put in such a position because of economics. You have every right to be angry, but don't let that anger sabotage your efforts in finding quality child care. The key issue here is one of control. You *do* have control over who will be with your children and under which circumstances.
2. You are beginning to wonder what happened to the old you. The end of the day finds you more than a little edgy, and the phrase "Is that all there is?" keeps running through your mind. Fatigue and depression seem to be the only things you can count on, day after day, with a new baby.
3. Your employer has made it clear that your job is in danger because of all the sick leave you have used. You're too intimidated to let him know that you use your sick leave to stay home when your child is ill or when the sitter leaves you hanging.
4. You or your husband's company has transferred the family to a new area. On top of everything else, you need to find before- and after-school care for the two older children and a nice grandmother-type for the baby when you finally do go back to work.
5. You've waited years for this baby. Your job is secure, and your husband hasn't stopped talking about the baby since you found out you were pregnant. Things could not be better! Grandma has offered to watch the baby full time after your three-month maternity leave, and you're just sure things will work out. Or will they? With all your eggs in one basket, it had better work out.

6. Through choice or by circumstance, you are a single parent. You need child care during the day while you work and occasionally on weekends or in the evening, but you don't know where to begin looking. Just thinking about interviewing a stranger gives you the chills. And what about pay? Just what is the going rate for a child care?

Each one of these families has a tremendous challenge ahead of them. Which situation do you most closely identify with? Do you see aspects of your situation in each example?

Now let's take a look at how everyone addressed their child care dilemma after a consultation with a child care consultant using a systematic approach to problem solving.

Julia. In this case, the consultant quickly realized that lack of information was Julia's biggest obstacle. Julia had settled for an unlicensed home based on convenience and economy. The dangers of placing a child, especially an infant, in an unlicensed home contributed greatly to Julia's anxiety and guilt. She simply did not have the time or the resources to make an informed search.

After taking the Self Test (see chapter 1), Julia realized that family day care homes were not the only option for the baby. Keeping the children together was non-negotiable; she felt strongly about having them all in the same place rather than all over town but didn't know how to accomplish this. Small family day care homes in California were licensed for six children, and she considered herself lucky to find an opening for *one* child. Julia's assumptions about child care centers were not realistic. For example, unaware that many child care centers offer discounts for more than one child, she assumed she couldn't afford to send all three of her children to a center.

This story does have a happy ending.

Julia discovered that the YMCA near her office has an infant center as well as a regular day care program. After several visits (before, during and after work), she realized the answer had been there all along. It was hard to find the time to explore the options, but the consultant pointed out that people take time off for dental appointments, why not for child care appointments? It was worth the extra effort. Now when her schedule permits, she is able to have lunch with the baby. The YMCA bus picks up the older kids after school as well as dropping them off in the morning. Julia says good-bye to all three children at 7:30 in the morning and picks them up at 5:15 on her way home in the afternoon. The program also provides vacation and summer programs, including field trips for the older kids. At last, Julia can get on with the business of rebuilding her life.

As a side benefit, Julia has met other single parents at the sign-out sheet and no longer feels like a stranger in a strange land. She has even taken advantage of several stress management classes offered by the Y.

The cost of the program was still more than she could afford, so having nothing to lose, Julia approached her employer for help and was delighted to learn that she could trade in her fitness club employee benefit in exchange for help with child care (see chapter 9: Employer-Sponsored Child Care).

Once the child care dilemma was solved, Julia was able to concentrate on her job with peace of mind. This resulted in a promotion and a substantial pay raise within a year.

Everyone is thriving.

Nancy. Once Nancy let down her guard with the child care consultant, numerous options became obvious. Few people can possibly know how a baby will affect their life until that baby is born. Nancy and Phil had unrealistic expectations about their roles and tremendous pressures to keep up appearances. Because they were financially secure, the first step was to hire a housekeeper to bring their home back to pre-baby standards. Once this was accomplished, arrangements were made for a housekeeper to come twice a week for a month, then once a week for the next six months.

Nancy's stamina was just not up to being able to deal with the repetition and energy required to perform household tasks *and* take care of the baby *and* be the beautiful hostess. She and Phil both felt strongly about raising their own child but lit up at the possibility of having a student come in during the afternoon several times a week in the beginning, so Nancy could work out at the health club or get caught up on sleep. Within a month, the baby was sleeping through the night and on a regular schedule with predictable naps and eating habits. Nancy cut back to once a week for her daytime workouts; two times a week Nancy worked out in the evening after Phil came home. Phil and the baby needed some time alone to get to know each other without Nancy hanging over Phil's shoulder.

At first Phil regarded these evenings as babysitting but soon came to look forward to this time with his son. He was getting pretty good at changing diapers and giving bottles. And because Phil knew which nights Nancy would be gone, he planned his schedule accordingly.

When emergencies arose or if Phil had to work late or Nancy wanted more time to herself, they were armed with a list of babysitters.

The consultant also suggested a new parent support group for Nancy where she met other "fast track" new mothers who were experiencing the same feelings she had. Nancy felt more comfortable discussing her concerns and fears with the others in the group rather than with her friends who she thought had expected so much of her. The person who was hardest on Nancy in terms of expectations was Nancy.

She also came to realize that babies are unlike business plans. As parents, we are thrust into this tremendous responsibility with no training whatsoever. For some people, it's sink or swim. Nancy was the kind of person who had to sink before she could swim.

When asked what advice she would pass along to other new parents, she replied with a quick smile, "Accept your limits, delegate tasks when possible, be flexible, and cultivate an amazing sense of humor."

Matt. Matt was a little more difficult to work with. His employer, taking advantage of a tax credit in the process, had provided the services of a child care consultant for employees who needed help. Matt's employer recognized the relationship between lack of adequate child care and productivity.

It wasn't until Matt's migraines became debilitating enough to require hospitalization for observation and tests that he faced up to his situation. He decided to be honest with his employer and risk his career rather than continue the charade.

You can imagine how relieved he felt upon receiving emotional support as well as having the services of the child care consultant. However, he was still pretty skeptical until he took the Self Test and realized that if he could deal with Monica's needs, then surely someone else could, also. Matt had to face the reality that he couldn't be all things at all times to his daughter. It wasn't healthy for her, and judging from his perspective in the hospital, it certainly wasn't healthy for him. Once he began to see the situation from a different point of view, he realized that his smothering was possibly hurting Monica's self-esteem. And Matt had to admit that he was really ready to make some changes.

With the help of the child care consultant, he hired a former registered nurse, about the same age as his mother, as a live-in nanny-housekeeper in exchange for room and board and an affordable salary. This freed Matt to concentrate on his work, date and still spend time with his daughter. Monica benefited from the arrangement as well. Her asthma attacks subsided dramatically within the first six months of the new arrangement, and because Matt was the employer rather than the son, he was able to make suggestions and garner feedback from the nanny in a way that had not been possible with his mother.

He has since become involved in the employee benefits council and is directly responsible for the formation of the "Brown Bag Lunch Bunch," an on-site support group that meets twice a month to discuss parenting issues. He has also been responsible for educating employees about the services of the company child care consultant *before* problems become crises.

Janet and Bill. Anyone spending more than five minutes with Janet and Bill would see what wonderful parents they make. Both are deeply committed to the welfare of their children; so when Janet considered her options after arriving in a new city, and discussed them with a child care consultant, it became obvious to the child care consultant that Janet would make an excellent child care provider. After the surprise wore off, Janet agreed to investigate the possibility.

Both Janet and Bill attended the orientation program for potential providers offered by their community care licensing agency. Janet also enrolled in a community service class on emergency first aid and child development offered through the local college. Following the guidelines given to them by the licensing agency, their home was licensed and ready to accommodate up to six children by the time school started. (Their children counted in the total allowed.) They decided to accept two full-time kids and one part-time child before and after school.

Janet's creativity was satisfied by program planning and implementation, the kids received excellent care in a nurturing environment, and Bill stayed involved by preparing a garden for the kids to plant and by helping on field trips. Word soon got out about this wonderful family day care home. Janet and Bill felt so sorry about turning people away that they compensated by offering the open slot to neighborhood kids on an emergency basis.

Everyone benefited!

Cynthia and Chuck. This couple required only one meeting with the child care consultant to put their minds at ease. Armed with the Self Test and information about how to find and evaluate different child care options, Cynthia felt better about her decision to have her mother care for their baby after it was born. If things didn't work out, she now had the tools to make an informed search for an alternative.

The consultant urged Cynthia to visit several family day care homes and infant centers *before* the baby was born and while she still had the stamina and an open mind.

They also discussed alternatives to traditional child care (see chapter 7). Once aware of the variety of options and confident in her ability to evaluate and choose what was best for them, Cynthia could relax with her decision.

Her eggs may have all been in one basket, but now she knew there were other baskets out there.

Dana. Family Court Services referred Dana to a child care consultant after Ben tried to legally take Robby away from her, citing her instability as grounds. They were also able to provide counseling referrals based on a sliding scale for emergency intervention and to put off hearing the case for three months to allow a "cooling off" period.

Ben perceived Dana as being unstable because she was experiencing a tremendous amount of stress, felt inadequate and was generally unhappy about the way things had turned out. Hers was not an unusual reaction under the circumstances, considering she was facing one trauma after another with no support system. Robby was the only one in the family getting his feelings out in the open, even though his misbehavior was considered antisocial.

Upon the advice of the child care consultant, the first thing Dana did was schedule an appointment with Robby's teachers at school to explain what was happening at home. She couldn't do anything to change the mind of the before- and after-school care program director but just talking with her helped Dana. The director did offer to take Robby back on a trial basis after he had been in therapy for three months. Once the teachers were aware of the problems at home, they were able to deal with Robby on a different level. He was not a bad kid—just an angry, unhappy little boy who missed having his mother and father together. However, there was still the problem of what to do with Robby before and after school while Dana worked.

Since he needed more individual attention at this point in his life, Dana felt uncomfortable having him in a center-based program with many other children. After extensive research, the child care consultant found a family day care home that had a low ratio of children. The provider's own children were almost all grown and gone except for her 16-year-old son who developed a special bond with Robby, having gone through the same experience at about the same age.

Robby slowly found other ways to release his anger, with the help of counseling and his new friend. The family day care home environment was the most stable part of Robby's day. This enabled him to cope with his still-shaky home life with his mother. There were fewer kids, more individual attention and more tolerance for negative behavior since the provider had experienced the same thing with her own son.

They were all still trying to find their way, but at least they had made a start in the right direction.

Homework

Answer the following questions on a separate sheet of paper.

If you are employed outside the home:

1. If I gave up my job, the thing I would miss most is:

2. My children benefit from my working in the following ways:

If you are not employed outside the home:

1. If I had quality, affordable child care, I would use the extra time to:

2. If I had quality, affordable child care, the amount of stress in my life would: be reduced, be increased or stay about the same.

For everyone:

1. When I was a child, I did/did not have child care.

2. My memories of that experience include:

3. List the qualities of a "good" parent and a "bad" parent.

BIBLIOGRAPHY

Anaheim Bulletin. Anaheim, Calif. March 31, 1989.

Hayward Review. Hayward, Calif. March 29, 1989.

Los Angeles Daily Journal. Los Angeles. April 13, 1989.

Moskowitz, M. and Townsend, C. "The Best Companies for Working Mothers." *Working Mother,* October 1989.

News Gazette. Martinez, Calif. April 8, 1989.

News Pilot. San Pedro, Calif. March 18, 1989.

USA Today. Washington, D.C. April 17, 1989.

3

DIFFERENT AGES/ DIFFERENT NEEDS

Each age has unique characteristics and special considerations. Based on the Self Test, if your newborn's ideal provider is a sedate grandmother-type, does that mean you'll have to change providers when that sweet angel turns into the "NO!" monster around her second birthday? The answer depends upon your child and the personality, stamina and sense of humor of the provider.

Everyone seems to have an opinion about what's best for your baby or child. They all make sense, too, based on the experiences of the advocate. The challenge is to listen objectively, weigh the pros and cons and make a rational decision based on your intuition and research. At the risk of oversimplifying, the following general guidelines are offered as a summary of characteristics to look for in a provider based on the age of your child.

The Infant

The infant thrives in an environment of loving—but not smothering—attention. You want someone who will change diapers promptly, make meal time pleasant and provide the right combination of cuddling and stimulation.

Dr. T. Berry Brazelton, a child development expert, feels strongly that the mother should stay home for at least the first four months after the baby's birth, if at all possible, for her sake as well as the baby's. In his opinion, this is the time during which babies develop patterns of communication with their faces and bodies. Given a choice, Dr. Brazelton advises the mother not to go back to work until she feels in control at home (I'm still waiting for that feeling) and then to begin by working part-time and gradually increasing her hours to full-time.

According to developmental specialist Erik Erikson, the first year of life is the age of trust versus mistrust. If the baby is well cared for and loved, it will learn that the world is a nice place to be.

Burton L. White, an expert in early childhood, feels that during the time from birth to crawling, parents (and providers) should work toward goals which include giving the baby a feeling of being loved and cared for as well as helping the infant develop an interest in the outside world. This can be done simply by changing the baby's scenery several times a day.

Many people choose in-home care for their infant because the baby stays in his own environment, is less exposed to childhood diseases and receives one-on-one care.

Family day care homes provide the same kinds of things in-home care provides except that there are other children around and the care is provided in someone else's home. This works well for families who have more than one child and want to keep the kids together. It also saves wear and tear on your own home. Check your area for licensing regulations. In California, for example, the ratio is one adult for four infants.

Many child care centers have an infant program. Advantages include convenience—if you choose a center near your office (which would make breast-feeding possible), and since most centers have educational requirements for their employees, you can be assured that your baby will receive supervised care by a trained provider.

Whether you choose an in-home provider, a family day care home or an infant center for your baby, look for someone who will hold your baby, talk to him, make lots of eye contact and possess a certain intuitiveness regarding your baby's temperament; someone who will allow your baby's individuality to develop into his own unique style. If the provider coos and talks to your infant during the interview, this is a good sign.

One last note about infants: Consistency is important at every age but especially around the age of four months when babies begin to recognize their favorite people and form strong attachments. Ideally, the provider is someone who is committed to their role for years to come. Realistically, you may find yourself changing providers as the needs of your family change. If you can avoid this during the first year, your baby will avoid the feelings of loss that occur when many changes are made. Many babies develop "stranger anxiety" at around seven months of age which would make introducing a new provider especially difficult at that time. So whatever your choice, I encourage you to research the options thoroughly—for your peace of mind as well as your baby's.

The Toddler

A toddler under age two needs constant supervision while exploring the world. You will want someone who will encourage exploration while maintaining a safe environment.

Developmental specialist Erik Erikson called this stage the era of autonomy versus shame and doubt. The toddler will be learning to walk, talk and explore. If she is encouraged to use initiative and independence and experiences consistent guidance, this increases her chances of being able to cope with situations requiring choice, control and autonomy.

Other experts call the period from 12 to 18 months the practicing months, when the toddler experiments with separation and begins to form more individuality. The period from 15 to 18 months until almost 24 months can be very trying as children alternate between independence and the safety of dependence. If your toddler is having a hard time adjusting to a new provider at this time, you might consider having the provider come to your home at times when you will also be there to give your child some added security.

In a center-based situation, ask to spend more time with your child to ease anxieties but *know when to go*. Many crying children stop crying within five minutes after the parent exits. This also applies to a family day care home. Most providers are anxious to work with the parents to make the experience for the toddler as positive as possible. Your toddler will thrive in a situation—whether in a child care center, in a family day care home or with an in-home provider—where she is encouraged to explore and where the provider keeps an eye on safety, possesses a good supply of stamina and patience and understands the duality of the young child learning a sense of independence amid unconditional love and acceptance.

The Two-Year-Old

Again, patience, stamina and a sense of humor are essential for anyone dealing with this age. Since some children also experience toilet training during this year, it is very important that the provider's ideas regarding this milestone closely match your own.

After discussions with my daughter's pediatrician, I learned that it is physically impossible, due to muscle development, for most children younger than age two to be toilet trained. This question came up during several interviews with potential providers who assured me that they could have Lyndsay trained by age one! When their references backed up the stories, it caused quite a bit of confusion on my part. These people weren't exaggerating. Training was going on, but they were the ones being trained to "catch" the child at the right times. The woman I eventually hired responded that toilet training was something that would happen through imitation and intuition with no set timetable. Her only preconceived idea about what worked involved a special shopping trip with Lyndsay to buy "big girl" panties preceding any attempt at toilet training. The last thing in the world Lyndsay wanted to do was to get her "big girl" panties wet.

This age requires much in terms of energy and creativity. If you've been using an in-home provider, now may be the time to review the job description and eliminate some of the light housekeeping to accommodate the demands of this age. For family day care homes and center-based care, this age can be especially challenging since the toddler wants to drift back to babyhood at some times while forging ahead at others. Fortunately, family day care homes and child care centers have the training, perspective and experience to deal with the needs of two-year-olds.

The Three-Year-Old to Five-Year-Old

The three-year-old benefits from being around other kids. Many children this age begin a part-time morning or afternoon preschool program. My daughter started in a program scheduled for two mornings a week for three hours each and graduated to five mornings at her own urging. I'll never forget the first time she brought home an art project or taught me the words to "Wheels on the Bus." She literally beamed at her independence! It was also nice to be able to see other children her age going through similar stages and to share ideas and discuss problems with other parents in the same boat as I.

If you've been using an in-home provider, determine if she will be responsible for locating such a program and whether she will provide transportation to and from the preschool.

A less formal approach would be to investigate the local library to see if it has a preschool story hour. Many parks and recreation departments and churches sponsor activities for this age group. Whatever you decide, keep the possibility open of combining an outside program with your regular child care, especially if your child has been relatively isolated up to this point. Since this is often the time a second child may be introduced into the family, the preschool child may have a hard time accepting a lot of changes at once. It may be comforting if the child remains in the same environment (preschool, family day care home) when the baby comes, but if you are just beginning preschool or a new provider, allow for a long period of adjustment. It would be better for everyone involved if the preschool or a new provider can be introduced before the new baby is born. Regression is normal during these times, so naturally you will want someone who will understand and provide nonjudgmental, unconditional support.

Some parents like the idea of in-home care until their children begin kindergarten. This is fine if that's what works for you, but kids this age—especially only children—also need regular exposure to other kids in order to begin the socialization process necessary for their adjustment to kindergarten. If you have a large family or close-knit neighborhood—lucky you! Most people have to look elsewhere.

The School-Age Child (Ages Six–12)

Once your child is in school, it may still be necessary to find before- and after-school care to accommodate your work schedule. The key to a good school-age program is good planning on the part of the provider. Look for a program that has age-appropriate activities and a good mix of quiet time as well as boisterous outside games that will allow children to blow off steam after maintaining control all day.

School-age children are in a good position to give you feedback concerning their care. In addition to checking whether or not your child's school offers before and after care, don't forget family day care homes in the area, parks and recreation departments and the local YMCA.

Some people make informal arrangements with friends or neighbors. This has the potential to backfire. Ask yourself if long periods of exposure will help or hurt your child's relationship with that person. If you are using your child's best friend's home, can their friendship take it? What happens when your child's best friend wants to have another friend over after school? Many children cannot handle the combination of three children playing together without having power struggles and hurt feelings.

Again, review your responses to the Self Test and research all options before making a decision.

WHEN IN DOUBT, TRUST YOUR INSTINCTS. You are the best judge of what's right for your child. The more you educate yourself on normal developmental stages, the easier it will be to make informed decisions regarding the care of your child. Certain ages present certain challenges, but ultimately it is your decision to choose the type of care your child will receive.

Homework

Visit two child care centers and two family day care homes within the next two weeks to compare and contrast these options. Reminder: Use a binder to hold your research materials (brochures, flyers and notes on site visits). This organizes your thoughts as well as accumulated paperwork, making a final decision easier.

BIBLIOGRAPHY

"Getting the Best Child Care—Other Than Mom." *U.S. News & World Report,* October 21, 1985, 70–71.

McNeil, Elton B. "Erikson and Personality." In *The Psychology of Being Human,* 96–97. San Francisco: Canfield Press, 1974.

McNeil, Elton B. "Erikson and Personality." In *The Psychology of Being Human*, 96–97. San Francisco: Canfield Press, 1974.

White, Burton L. *The First Three Years of Life*. New York: Avon Press, 1975.

Yeiser, Lin. *Nannies, Au Pairs, Mothers' Helpers—Caregivers*. New York Vintage Books, 1987.

4
IN-HOME CARE

In-home care may be defined as a provider caring for your child in *your* home. It may also be defined as someone who provides care for someone else's child (or children) in *their* home. In either case, a license is usually not required for this service unless the provider is caring for more than one family's children on a regular basis. (See state-by-state resource list starting on page 119 for specifics on your state's regulations, or call your state's Department of Social Services for detailed information.)

In-home care can fill the void felt by many who do not have a large extended family to call upon for child care. Gone are the days of three generations living under one roof. Once upon a time, Grandma or Aunt Louise was as likely to scold you for acting up as Mom, but no more.

Advantages and Disadvantages

In-home care offers many advantages for parents and children, including:

Simple logistics: It's much easier to get out the door in the morning if the provider is coming to your home, rather than if you are packing up a day's worth of supplies and dressing, feeding and hurrying your child along—all the while trying not to sound like a drill sergeant—and making that stop at the provider's before beating the clock to work. When care is given in your home, you don't necessarily have to do a load of wash the night before if your child needs an extra change of clothes for the day care center. In fact, you can include light housework in the job description for your in-home provider. Many parents have the provider come 30 minutes early to prepare breakfast for the children—allowing them a chance for an uninterrupted shower. This makes for a nice exit with unhurried hugs and kisses given to kids in pajamas.

Sick child care: In many states, including California, child care centers cannot legally admit sick children. What do you do when you have an important meeting at 8:15 A.M. and your child has a temperature of 103 degrees at 7:15? Many family day care homes will care for your sick child in an isolated area, but there's nothing like being in your own bed when you have the sniffles.

Control: By hiring an in-home provider, you can control the type of person responsible for the care of your child. You intrinsically know the ideal person for your family, whether that be a grandmother-type, a college student with lots of energy or a person who most closely resembles your parenting style. *You* make the final decision and have control over your house rules.

One-on-one care: There was a period of time when my daughter Lyndsay was extremely aggressive around other children. In spite of all efforts, she continued to pick on kids (both smaller and larger than herself) to the point of being asked not to return to our Mom & Toddler class. Lisa, our in-home provider was the calm head that prevailed during this test. As a parent, it was very difficult for me to see that this was a temporary situation. Needless to say it was rougher on me than it was on Lyndsay. But Lisa had the perspective to know it was Lyndsay's way of expressing her needs—something I had trouble seeing, especially after the experience with the toddler group. Lisa was able to give Lyndsay the one-on-one attention she needed to get through this period (for some reason, the more attention I gave to her, the worse the situation became). Lisa also made it possible for me to get away from the situation for short periods of time. That way, I could step back and see things more clearly. Under those circumstances, I would not have been comfortable with Lyndsay in a family day care home or child care center because their concern is the welfare of the children as a group, and as we saw first hand, if one child consistently upsets the group, she has to go.

Familiar surroundings: Your kids will still be able to play with their neighborhood friends, either at your home or the home of the friend. In-home care is the closest thing to having Mom at home when Mom isn't home. Your kids can bake cookies, fold towels fresh from the dryer and do homework—all at their own pace.

Compatible activities: An in-home provider can take the kids to their ballet lessons, soccer practice or library story hour. Your children do not have to alter their interests to fit with your work schedule. This can eliminate a tremendous amount of stress.

Another adult to love: If your child is having a difficult time with a transition, having another adult to love can provide stability. As in a family day care home, an in-home provider can be a confidant, a soft shoulder, a buffer between the child and the parent and a safe harbor during times of stress. This is especially true in single family homes. It's gratifying to hear your child refer to the provider as "my Lisa" or "Grammy Jane."

Disadvantages to using an in-home provider include:

Lack of privacy: On those days where you're the one with the sniffles, life goes on around you. If your children are in a child care center of family day care home, you can sneak home for a nap when you feel a cold coming on or join your husband for a lunch or early dinner rendezvous. Even stopping by the house to pick up a forgotten report or umbrella becomes more than a two-minute stop because you often can't just run in and out without acknowledging your child and provider.

Wear and tear on the house: Even if you include light housework in the job description, there will be days when it doesn't get done because the kids need extra time. Nothing is more discouraging than to walk into a dirty house at the end of the day while holding two bags of groceries for dinner. The provider's first responsibility is, of course, the children. Consider, though, that your carpeting will last longer if your children are in a family day care home or child care center—not to mention the furniture, toys and all the other things used on a daily basis that will last longer.

Expense: Depending on the area, in-home care can be costly compared to family day care homes or a child care center. More on costs will be discussed later.

Isolation of the provider: Burnout is common but fortunately avoidable. Careful screening and honest on-going communication will reveal the burnout factor in your provider. The trick is to know the symptoms and intervene before problems begin.

FINDING AN IN-HOME PROVIDER

Once you've weighed the pros and cons and decided to try an in-home provider for your child, where do you begin the search?

Word of mouth is the most obvious place to start. Let *everyone* know you're looking for a reliable, loving in-home provider for your child. Mention it to the secretary at your child's school, at PTA meetings, at work, at the tennis club, or at your own school. You never know when you'll make that connection. You might be surprised by how many people know a provider or can refer you to a resource that will help. Even if the butcher at your favorite grocery store can't think of anyone at the time, perhaps his niece will stop by over the weekend and complain about not having a summer job. Bingo! Guess who he'll think about?

In one case, Linda ran an ad in the newspaper for an in-home provider and shared the applicants with her next-door neighbor who ended up hiring Linda's second choice! The neighbor benefited from Linda's screening process, and Linda benefited by having someone to bounce ideas and concerns off of. They both found excellent people for their children.

How to Write a Classified Ad That Get Results!

The key to a successful ad in the paper is to be *as specific as possible*. The Self Test has already narrowed down your expectations and requirements, so writing the ad should be relatively easy. Begin by reviewing the results of the Self Test. Next, check out what other people have done by studying the ads under "Child Care" or "Mother's Helper" or "Nanny." The following are examples of typical ads:

- **Child care. Rosemont area. Own transportation. 555-0000.** These folks saved a lot of money by condensing their ad to the bare minimum. The problem is, they left out the majority of the information needed. They will probably get calls from just about everyone.
- **Child care. My Rancho Cordova home, 2 children, 4–5 days/wk. Non smoker. 555-0000.** This is better—at least we know how many children but what age? Which days? Can I take a bus to get there, or do I need transportation to take the kids to lessons?
- **Child care. Part-time, Monday, Wednesday, Friday from 9:00–2:30, flex. nights and wkends. 555-0000.** This one started out great by defining the exact hours needed, but what does the second half of the ad mean? Are nights and weekends required or optional? How many kids and what ages?
- **Child care. Professional couple seeks loving mother's helper Monday, Tuesday and Wednesday 7:30 A.M.–6:30 P.M. for 2 preschoolers in our Carmichael home. Inc. light housekeeping. Experience with children and reliable transportation required. Great work environment. Salary + benefits. Ideal for parents, seniors and students. 555-0000, leave message before 6 P.M.** This ad has a lot going for it: It's full of information, uses adjectives and encourages the reader to call to find out about the great work environment, salary and benefits (they live in a beautiful home with pool and other amenities, pay well and include vacation and sick leave after a 6-month probation period). It also screens out people without experience or transportation and recruits a wide variety of people such as seniors, students and parents. These are people who may not have considered this type of work before, even though they have the experience. This ad also has an air of professionalism to it.

Your goal is to write an ad that will automatically screen people who are not qualified yet entice those who are, to respond!

Really put some thought into the wording of your ad. You should have several rewrites before you finally call the newspapers. In addition to the papers in your city, you might also consider putting the ad in several church bulletins (check the yellow pages for churches in your area) as well as at student employment centers at local colleges and universities. Other resources for your ad may be the local "Penny Saver" ads that are delivered free to homes throughout the area. Check the yellow pages under "Newspapers."

Now that you've placed the ad, are your palms getting sweaty just thinking about talking to all those strangers (some stranger than others)? Exactly how do you tell the difference between a mass murderer and the next potential member of your family *over the telephone?* Relax. There are ways. But first let's talk about how to prepare for the first day of the ad.

What to Expect. Be prepared for a lot of desperate people to call—people who are not qualified, non-English speakers and mothers who call for their grown children in order to get them employed and out of the house, to name just a few. Lots of different people pore over the want ads with their morning coffee. If you expect to hear from some unusual people, you won't get discouraged when they do call.

Be sure to ask about the best days to run this type of ad when calling it in to the newspaper. In my experience, Sunday and Monday ads get a good response. Possibly more people turn to the want ads over a leisurely cup of coffee with the rest of the Sunday paper or wake up on Monday morning to the realization that they still don't have employment.

One other hint I found helpful concerns the length of the run. The nice people at the *Sacramento Bee* suggested I take advantage of the five-day run rate but cancel the ad after just three days if I got a good response (I did!).

Also be prepared for a large number of calls. A well-written ad can generate 20 to 30 calls a day!

How can you possibly talk to that many people—especially if you work outside the home?

Your Answering Service: Voice Mail or an Answering Machine

Now is the time to subscribe to voice mail through your local telephone company or buy an answering machine. Not only will you be able to take calls without being home, but your privacy will be protected during those times when a phone call would be disruptive. Even though you may specify in the ad to call before 6:00 P.M., some people will breeze right over that part or be so excited about the job that they can't wait to talk to you. Your outgoing message might be something like this:

"Hi. Thanks for calling. If you're calling about the ad in the paper, please leave your name, telephone number and the best time for me to reach you—as well as any personal information that will help me get to know you—at the sound of the beep. I'll be returning calls between 7:00 and 9:00 P.M. daily. Thanks for calling, and don't forget to wait for the beep!"

Another advantage to using a telephone answering machine is that it saves having to tell people you've filled the position long after the ad has stopped running:

"Hi. Thanks for calling. If you're calling regarding the ad in the paper, the position has been filled. Good luck in your search, and thanks again for your interest!"

For some reason, calls trickle through for about a week after the ad has stopped running in the newspaper.

The disadvantages of using an answering machine are relatively few. Some people simply will not leave a message because they don't want to sound silly. Plus, your friends may get irritated when they try to reach you and keep getting a recorded message. But all in all, it's worth serious consideration.

If at all possible, try to list a phone number to call rather than a post office box to respond to in your ad. This may be difficult if you are trying to replace an unsatisfactory provider who is still in your employ. If that's the case, do you have a friend who would be willing to take messages for you at her phone number? The reason post office boxes don't draw the response a telephone number does is because you'll lose people who don't have a resume or the time to develop one, have no access to a typewriter or lack the resources to have a resume typed.

Generally, it's also not a good idea to take calls at work because it's time-consuming and disruptive, not to mention distracting.

Handling Calls. If you are getting only a handful of calls from unqualified people, it's time to reword the ad or place it elsewhere.

Before the first day of the ad, take a sheet of paper and divide it into columns to create a form to be filled out on all qualified applicants. It can be as simple as "Name," "Telephone Number" and "First Impressions" or may resemble a job application, as the following example illustrates:

The Telephone Log

Date: _____

Name: _____

Address (or nearest cross street): _____

Telephone number and best times to call: _____

_____

Own transportation? Reliable? DMV printout available? (In California, you may request a Department of Motor Vehicle printout listing tickets and accidents, which is a good idea if part of the job includes driving your children on a regular basis.) _____

Previous experience, including most-recent child care position:_____

_____

_____

Last job, if not related to child care: _____

Reason for job search: _____

_____

Seeking full-time, part-time, flexible hours? _____

Will your own child be included in care? _____

Hours/days available? _____

Prefer to work in own home, our home, no preference? _____

Salary requirement range: _____

What are your future goals: _____

_____

What is your favorite age group and why? _____

Do you swim (if your home has a pool) or have allergies (if you have a pet)? _____

Comments: _____

_____

References (Ask for three names and phone numbers if you're certain you'll be interviewing the respondent in person later.): _____

Follow-up: _____

The first part is self-explanatory but before you even get into your listed questions, you might begin by asking why they responded to *your* ad? This is a good icebreaker.

You'll want to know where they live because even if they *swear* that transportation is not a problem, if they live more than 10 miles away, this may be a consideration if it gets down to two candidates and one lives only three blocks away.

Are they looking for full-time, part-time or flexible hours? There is no right or wrong answer here—just a judgment as to whether or not your needs match.

Asking about the salary requirements up front saves a lot of time if their needs do not match your budget. What if they ask you about the salary first? You might try turning their question around by asking what their requirements are:

Them: "Do you mind if I ask what you pay?"
You: "Not at all. What are your salary requirements?"

Chances are if they answer with a lower figure, you can adjust your range.

Them: "My last job paid $550 a month. My needs have changed, and I need at least $625."
You: "The salary range is $625–800 a month after one year."

This makes everyone happy. Little did the applicant know that you paid your last provider $750 a month at the beginning and regretted topping out so quickly. This meets the needs of the provider while still allowing room for raises and staying within your budget.

Asking about the future goals of the applicant gives you a better idea of who they are and where they are headed. It also helps you gauge their longevity with your family. The college freshman who is willing to work her classes around your schedule may be a good investment compared to the person who isn't sure what they want or where they'll be a year down the road.

The question regarding their favorite age group turns up some interesting responses, too. They don't have to list your child's age as their favorite. I once had an applicant talk about the sheer joy and curiosity a two-year-old displays on a rainy afternoon and even though my daughter was only six-months-old at the time, that answer gave me a lot of information about that person.

Only ask for references if you're sure you want to interview this applicant in person later.

In the section for follow-up, list any reminders such as "refer to Caroline" if this person doesn't meet your needs but you know someone who may be just right for them, or "call for back-up, evening or weekend care" in case they are right in all ways but can't fit into your schedule.

By the way, this is an excellent way to find occasional babysitters—ask them if they are interested in this as an alternative.

Make your telephone log as detailed or general as you wish, as long as you're comfortable with the information it provides.

You will want to ask all applicants the same basic questions but feel free to digress if something else interests you. I once spent 30 minutes talking with a woman who had extensive experience with autistic children. The first 10 minutes we talked about the position, the last 20 about autism. Don't be afraid to be curious.

Once you've organized your telephone log into a set of questions and summary of information, have 50 copies made at the local copy shop, and you're all set for the first phone call!

In addition to the telephone log, have a copy of the ad taped to the clipboard to review the basic requirements of the job. Again, you'd be surprised how many people respond to ads without thoroughly reading the requirements. Get this out of the way first, so you won't waste your time (not to mention your voice):

Them: "Hi. I'm calling about the ad in the paper."

You: "Oh, good. Thanks for calling. I assume you live in the Carmichael area, have your own transportation, don't smoke, won't be bringing a child with you and are available for long-term employment beginning in June?"

Them: "Well, actually I was hoping to bring my nine-month-old son along—he's real quiet."

You: "I'm sorry, that arrangement isn't what I'm looking for, but good luck to you."

This may sound cold to you, but remember, you've put a lot of work into defining your needs—*don't let anyone change them for their convenience. Remember, there is someone out there who is qualified and available—don't waste time on those who are not.* The exception is if the person sounds wonderful but simply can't conform to the requirements of the job. In that case, go ahead and finish the telephone interview and make a referral in case you run into someone who is looking for just such a provider. Networking never ends.

If the caller meets the requirements of your ad, ask her to tell you something about herself before you launch into your telephone log questions. For those on the shy side, you may need to ask a few questions to get them started, but avoid questions that require a simple yes or no response. The question about their favorite age group is a good icebreaker. If you like what you hear, go ahead with the other questions on the telephone log and answer the caller's questions about the job.

Remember—you have a right to ask personal questions relative to their ability to perform the job to your specifications. They expect it.

Some red flags to watch for include:

- A desperate quality to their questions
- An emphasis on money
- A "superior" attitude
- Personal problems
- A gut feeling that this isn't the right one

You're probably wondering how you can judge whether or not a person is right for your child over the telephone. The answer is easy: You can't. The only way to do that is during a personal interview. The telephone interview will screen people who are *not* right for the position and provide applicants for a personal interview.

You're not making any decisions during the telephone interview. You are merely judging whether or not there is potential for a personal interview.

Your last question should be, "Can you think of anything I've left out that you'd like me to know?"

The telephone interview may last anywhere from 30 seconds for the wrong person to 10 to 15 minutes for someone who has a lot of potential. In closing, tell everyone that the ad is running until Thursday (or whenever), at which time you'll call back only those people you want to interview in person. Stress that if they don't get a call back, it's because you have enough for the first round of interviews. Thank them for their interest and try to end on an "up" note. By letting them know *you'll call them*, hopefully they won't pester you with phone calls to see if you made up your mind yet.

After the first 10 or so calls, you will begin to feel like an old pro and become better at identifying qualified applicants. Of course, after the third day, you may get sick of hearing your own voice parrot the same questions. Almost before you know it, the worst is over and you're ready to set up personal interviews with the cream of the crop!

The Personal Interview

Don't worry about how the house looks. In fact, the closer it looks to the normal state of things, the better.

Do not offer coffee or snacks, and keep socializing down to small talk preceding the actual interview. In other words, treat this as you would any business interview.

When setting up the interview, specify how long it will last. ("I have 45 minutes on Monday at 3:00 for our interview—is that convenient?")

If at all possible, have the child there during part of the interview. It's a good idea to invent a reason to leave the room (but stay within earshot) to observe how your child relates to this person.

Your clipboard will come in handy again, with a list of prearranged questions (see samples).

Talk about family and work situations briefly, but be specific about which duties and responsibilities you expect the provider to perform. You already know a little about this person from the telephone interview, so now is the time to follow up with more detailed questions.

Interview at least five people before making a decision. Then set up a second interview with the top two people. Even if you feel confident about someone, don't make any decisions until you've talked to everyone and completed a second interview with your first choice. Believe me, it's easy to get carried away with excitement at finding someone who seems perfect. A second interview gives the rest of the family, including your husband, a chance to meet the applicant and gives you a chance to check references.

Speaking of references, if you did not ask for references during your telephone interview, ask the applicant to bring a list of three references with phone numbers along. Some people like to talk to the references before they talk to the applicant, others like to do it the other way around; it's up to you. I prefer to meet the applicants first because if I don't feel comfortable with them, it doesn't matter what the references say.

SAMPLE QUESTIONS FOR APPLICANTS

What is it about this type of work that interests you?
How long have you been doing this type of work?
Discuss your previous experience with children.
Medical background—any barriers to performing typical duties?
Personal goals?
What is the most important thing to remember when dealing with children?
What would you do if my child hit another child?
What would you do if my child refused to obey you?
Are you willing to make a six-month commitment? One year?
What do you think your references will say about you?
Discuss your feelings on diet and give examples of typical meals and snacks.
What are your discipline methods? Do you have a problem with any of my ground rules?
What would you do if my child made you angry?

How much TV is too much?

Do you have experience with toilet training?

What is a good age to begin toilet training? Describe the method you would use.

What is the most frustrating thing about kids?

How many times did you miss work last year due to illness?

Are you able to work overtime in an emergency?

Do you know CPR or would you be willing to learn?

How would you fill the hours during the summer when the kids are out of school?

What type of field trips would you like to take the kids on?

Do you want to be called for extra hours in the evening and on weekends, or do you prefer to keep your off-hours free?

Tips

Before you interview the first candidate, spend an hour brainstorming for questions to ask during the interview. Don't worry about how personal or silly they seem.

During the interview, try not to "feed" answers to your own questions ("you don't approve of spanking, do you?"). You want genuine responses.

If things are going well at this point, you may want to review any restrictions such as telephone usage, visitors, smoking and so forth. Now is the time to discuss salary and work schedules.

Again, don't make any decisions until you've had a chance to interview all the applicants and check references.

To signal the end of the interview, ask if there is anything they'd like to add. If not, stand and stretch out your hand to thank them and let them know when you'll be calling for a second interview by saying something like this:

"I have four more people to talk to before Monday when I'll be calling back the top two for a second interview. You'll hear from me one way or the other by Monday night."

As a common courtesy, the people who participated in the personal interview should be called even if they are not chosen; they deserve to be treated professionally.

Follow these guidelines for the rest of the personal interviews, then give yourself a day to call references. This is one of the most important aspects of finding good people, yet many people skip this step because: "It's too much trouble." "People just say what you want to hear anyway." "I don't know what to ask." Review the following list of sample questions for references before you pick up the phone, and it may make the task a little easier. Before you begin questioning the reference, introduce yourself and state the reason for the call:

"Hi. My name is _____. Lisa Andrews listed you as a character reference. She has applied for a job with me as a child care provider for my three-year-old son. Do you have a few minutes to talk, or is there a better time for me to call back?"

If they have the time to talk, jump right in with any of the following questions as well as your own.

SAMPLE QUESTIONS FOR REFERENCES

When did Lisa work for you and in what capacity?
How long did she work for you?
What are your children's ages?
What would you say Lisa's strongest traits are?
What areas could use some improvement?
How many times was Lisa late? Sick? Did she call first?
How much TV was watched when Lisa was there?
Describe her responsibilities. Was housework included?
Did she ever have to deal with an emergency while working for
     you? What was it, and how did she handle it?
What was Lisa's salary? (They may be more comfortable with giv-
     ing you a range.)
Why did she leave?
What do your kids say about her now that she's gone? In what
     ways do they miss her?
What do your kids say was the most and least fun about her?
Do you know of any reason I shouldn't hire her?
How did your parenting style blend with Lisa's personality?
Was her car reliable?
Did you feel comfortable when Lisa was there?

These are only suggestions to get you started. Choose as many as you want and *write down the answers!* It's hard to remember things when you've talked to 15 different people.

Record the following information on your clipboard right next to the information based on the telephone interview, personal interview and reference check. Review everything and then sleep on it. Put it out of your mind for a day to give your subconscious a chance to digest the information.

Conclusions

What is my lasting impression?

Did this person seem loving and kind and genuinely concerned with the welfare of my child? Or did they seem motivated by money?

Describe the applicant to a third person.

Can I imagine this person caring for my child?

Do I have a sense of trust about this person?

How did my child react to them?

What are my reservations?

Did they seem intimidating to me with firm ideas of how children should be raised, or were they receptive to my values?

Did they ask good questions? Any questions?

Will I have to compromise in any way if I hire them?

Am I settling for someone I don't want due to a poor response to the ad?

It's normal to have reservations—especially if you feel forced to find child care, but try to distinguish between normal feelings of hesitation and self-sabotage.

Trust your instincts but be sure to check references.

A Word About Rates of Pay

Rates of pay vary from place to place. Some places, like the student employment office at my local college, will not accept a job listing unless minimum wage is paid. Some people pay by the day, week or month. The federal government is interested in your arrangement as well—especially if you take a child care deduction on your income taxes or employ in-home caregivers. To be safe, check with your local Internal Revenue Service office. They will send you a brochure with information. Don't forget state disability, social security and worker's compensation insurance. Your homeowner's insurance policy may cover worker's compensation, so check with your agent.

Play it safe and play it smart: Ask about state and federal guidelines for employers, because that's what you are. Don't take a chance by paying under the table, especially if this is someone who will be with you for a long time. It can only come back to haunt you later.

In determining rates of pay many things must be considered: the number of children and their ages, whether housework is included, hours (early morning or late evening hours merit more money), your own budget and fair market wages. You can find out what fair market wages are by calling other people who use child care (check the classified ads) and asking them what they pay. Most people will be happy to share that information with you if you explain the situation. If your provider has a salary requirement, that's obviously another consideration.

Some people pay their top salary right from the beginning to entice quality people. I'd rather give a salary range with the understanding that raises will be given every three months until the top range is reached and yearly thereafter. While discussing salary, also mention bonuses at Christmas, whether or not sick leave and vacation may be accrued and, if so, at what rate and after how long a trial period. Discuss the possibility of taking the provider along on vacations as a benefit.

We took our provider to Hawaii twice. Each time we paid all expenses in exchange for approximately four hours of child care per day and evening care when we went out. We even hired a hotel sitter one night, so we could take our provider out on the town for doing such a great job!

The rate of pay should be fair, affordable, consistent with the market and have room to grow, either in amount or benefits. If you are unable to give regular raises, consider expanding benefits such as extra time off with pay during finals week for students or an occasional three day weekend off with pay.

By the way, it makes a lasting impression to remember your provider on Mother's Day with a card from your children. If they are very young, you can always cheat and sign their names for them. I promise you it will leave a nice impression.

Always treat your provider like a professional.

AFTER YOU OFFER AND THEY ACCEPT

Now that you've hired an in-home provider there are some things that can be done to ease the transition for everyone.

Preparing Your Child

Explain to your child why a provider will be coming to your home. If you work outside the home, explain why you work and try to convey a positive feeling about what you do. Whether the provider is part-time relief so you can attend school or maintain your sanity or full-time permanent, don't relay a feeling of guilt about it. If you expect your kids to have a hard time adjusting, chances are they won't let you down. Be encouraging! Remind them that they've already met the provider during the interview and refresh their memory about how nice that person was.

Explain what time you'll be leaving and what time you'll be back. "Right after *Sesame Street*" is a lot easier for a child to understand than the concept of 6:00.

Tell your child what to expect while the provider is there, and take a little extra time the first week or so in the morning to avoid rushing out the door the minute the provider arrives. *Never* force a child to approach the provider. Let the child set the pace for the relationship.

If possible, have the provider come for a few hours on a day when you'll be home to help the child get used to this new person. This will also give you a chance to show the provider where everything is in the house.

Be tolerant of any negative behavior as your child adjusts to the new routine. I remember a little girl named Amy who told her mom she didn't like the new provider, a college student with lots of smiles and energy. Amy wanted her old provider (a sweet grandmother) back. Sounds perfectly normal, doesn't it? Mom panicked and replaced the new provider with someone more like the old one (the former provider had moved out of town, so it was impossible to get her back). The next week Amy was complaining about the new provider and wanted to know what happened to the "fun girl!" The moral of the story? Allow for a transition period before making any changes.

Another good idea is to tape record the child's favorite story to be played before nap time along with a confident reassurance.

Preparing Your Provider

Use a three-ring binder as a communication center and include the following information:

- ❖ The provider's job description, including daily, weekly and monthly responsibilities
- ❖ Emergency information (see page 43)
- ❖ A typical day for your child
- ❖ Any food dislikes, bedtime routines, meal schedules
- ❖ Acceptable discipline methods
- ❖ Daily activities, such as reading to them for one-half hour a day before bed or letting them splash in the wading pool as a reward for good behavior

Ask the provider to use this communication center to keep you up to date on cute things said during the day, unusual fussiness, grocery lists, reminders, requests.

Older children can use this communication center to ask if friends can come over after school, remind you about an open house or share the latest joke.

Also fill out and keep the following information in your three-ring binder to be used by your in-home provider in case of emergencies:

Emergency Information/Medical Instructions

Parent/Guardian: Please check line 1 or line 2 to indicate action desired in the event of an accident or emergency.

1. _____ In the event of an accident or other emergency, when a parent/guardian is unavailable, I hereby authorize_____ _____ to make such arrangements as he/she deems necessary for my child to receive medical or hospital care, including necessary transportation. Under such circumstances, I further authorize the physician named below to undertake such care and treatment of my child as he/she considers necessary. In the event said physician is not available, I authorize such care and treatment to be performed by any licensed physician or surgeon.

The undersigned hereby agrees to bear all costs incurred as a result of the foregoing.

Physician's Name _____

Phone number _____

Insurance Carrier _____

Policy number _____

2. _____ I do not choose the above statement and desire the following action _____

_____

_____

_____

Child's Name _____

Parent/Guardian _____

Signature _____

Date _____

Emergency Information No Home
Should Be Without

Because even the most reliable provider can become flustered during an emergency, it's important to have the following information organized on a separate sheet of paper and mounted in a prominent place such as on the refrigerator or near the telephone.

1. Parents' names, address and home telephone number. (Many homes no longer have the telephone number mounted on the phone. You also don't want the provider to have to run outside to get the address off the house in an emergency.)
2. Names of all the children, birthdates and approximate weights (update regularly).
3. Pediatrician's name and telephone number.
4. Hospital emergency room telephone number and address along with directions for the best way to get there.
5. Poison control center's local number. (Check the first page of your telephone directory or call information for this number. Of course, in an emergency, call 911.) *Be sure to tell the provider to keep the bottle or container of the suspected poison and bring it to the emergency room if the child is taken there.*
6. Location of syrup of ipecac if, AND ONLY IF, the provider is instructed to induce vomiting. Check the expiration date on the bottle and review instructions on how to administer it with the provider. Many people don't know it has to be taken with lots of water.
7. Nearby friend or neighbor to call as a backup in case you can't be reached.
8. Medical insurance information, including policy number and name of carrier.
9. Police and fire department telephone numbers.
10. Children's allergies, strong likes and dislikes, bedtime routine (leave door open, night-light on, etc.).
11. Work number for Mom *and* Dad.

It's a good idea to play "what if" with your children and provider. "What if someone broke into the house while you were home?" "What if one of the kids was choking on a hot dog?" "What if you couldn't find the parents or the backup in an emergency?" "What if there was a fire and you had to evacuate the house—where would you gather?"

Everyone should complete an emergency first aid course including CPR.

Preparing Yourself

Ideally, you've found someone with whom you are very comfortable, so why do you still have this knot in the pit of your stomach?—because you're normal and because you're a good parent. It's okay to feel nervous at first. After all, you don't *really* know this person yet. Give yourself a break—don't try to be brave. Tell your provider something like, "I know things will work out great, but I'll feel better if I call you once in the morning and once in the afternoon to check on things. It doesn't mean I don't trust you—it's just what I have to do to be comfortable." Of course, she'll understand.

You have a transition period of your own to go through whether you recognize it or not. And yours may be the toughest to deal with because you're busy helping everyone else.

But what if the kids like the new provider too much?

I remember the first time we went to Hawaii with Lyndsay and Lisa. My husband and I flew there a week early to spend some time alone while Lisa and Lyndsay arrived later. Lyndsay's first night on the island was filled with fear, jet lag and confusion. Did she call for Mom in the middle of the night? Nope. It was Lisa's name she called. My gut feeling was agony until I realized that she had just spent a week without me and had cemented the bond with Lisa. As soon as I realized what a blessing this was to have someone my child could feel that close to, I felt better. It took almost a week before Lyndsay was her old self around me again (could a 15-month-old child harbor resentment over being abandoned?).

It's normal to feel a twinge of envy about the relationship your children may develop with a provider. After all, he or she gets to stay home all day with them while you work—who wouldn't feel cheated at times? However, if these feelings are more than fleeting or occur with regularity, maybe it's time to talk with someone about what's happening—your husband, a woman friend, a minister or a mental health professional. A little jealousy is normal, especially in the beginning. It's part of the process for some people but shouldn't be a daily occurrence.

The Trial Period

It's a good idea to establish a trial period after which the parent and the provider sit down to discuss whether or not to continue the arrangement. This can be done on a formal basis, such as including it in the job description, or on an informal basis. Two weeks to one month is usually long enough to evaluate how things are going. Don't be too quick to get rid of the provider if there are problems—especially if your kids are crazy about her but she's having a hard time getting to your house on time. Perhaps the problems can be worked out. This is the time to talk about it. Maybe it's a matter of adjusting the start and stop times. The idea is to communicate how you feel while in a safe environment, and the post-trial period conference is the time to do it.

The Employment Agreement

It's a good idea to spell out everything you expect of a provider—job duties, length of trial period, overtime policy, rate of pay, and so forth—to avoid confusion and prevent misunderstandings. Count on at least two drafts before the final agreement (see sample). Don't forget things like sick leave and/or vacation benefits, including days when you are ill or on vacation. Do they still get paid? These are the details that can complicate your life unless you deal with them before they arise.

The Employment Agreement

This agreement is entered into between _____ and _____ for the purpose of defining and clarifying child care job duties and expectations. It is understood that on _____, after a trial period of _____ weeks/months, all parties will evaluate the situation, review the agreement and revise terms as necessary.

Starting salary is _____ to be increased to _____ after a trial period lasting _____ weeks/months. Regular increases will be considered on a _____ basis. Overtime will be paid for any hours above the agreed upon terms with a 30-minute per week grace period for the parent to allow for minor delays. Overtime will be paid to the nearest hour thereafter. It is the responsibility of the parent as an employer to withhold necessary taxes. Vacation and sick leave is earned during the first six months but not usable until the seventh month of employment at a rate of _____. In the event that the provider is ill or unable to perform the duties, it is the responsibility of the parent/provider to secure a replacement for that day. Time off for either the provider or the parent must be requested a reasonable time in advance to allow alternate plans to be made. A gas allowance is/is not paid to the provider for furnishing transportation to and from activities involving the children. This rate is _____ per _____ mile/week. In the case of incompatibility, a better job offer, or unforeseen circumstances on the part of the provider, the provider agrees to give a two-week notice to allow time for the parents to find a replacement.

In the case of termination due to misrepresentation on the part of the provider, any salary owed him/her may be used to defray the cost of finding a replacement. If the safety and well-being of the children is at risk, this agreement may be terminated immediately by the employer.

Job Duties

In addition to providing quality care for the children, the provider will include the following light housework in his/her job:

Detailed Daily Housework: (as, have house picked up by the time parents come home from work, dishes done and laundry folded)

Detailed Weekly Housework: (grocery shopping on Friday, vacuum living room twice a week, one day being Friday, three loads of laundry a week)

Detailed Monthly Housework:

Child Care:

A typical day with my child:

Extra Child Care Responsibilities: (drive to soccer practice, supervise swimming during the summer, drive to preschool three days a week, etc.)

Discipline: The following method of discipline is to be used with my child:

Policy on use of phone by provider, meals, visitors, smoking, and anything else you feel strongly about:

Is the provider available or interested in extra hours not in the employment agreement? If yes, which extra hours are available?

As you can see, you can get as detailed as you want with an employment agreement, but remember that's all this is: an *agreement* to help avoid misunderstandings before they occur. I doubt it would hold up in court because that's not what it's meant to do. The Employment Agreement is a tool to use with your provider to start out on the right foot.

Obviously you'll want to use your own priorities rather than adopt this sample agreement verbatim. But it should give you a good place to start.

Other Uses for In-Home Providers

Consider using a younger person if you plan to be home. I found a teenager who would stop by on a regular basis to play with the baby while I slept, read or worked on a special project. They didn't seem to get as tired of "peek-a-boo" as I did, and they loved to shower the baby with attention. Sometimes a walk around the block with someone new can give everyone the break they need.

Next time you have a dinner party, why not have the provider come to the house? You'll be able to get ready a lot faster with someone entertaining the little ones, bathing them and keeping them occupied so you can enjoy your guests. An added bonus would be to have them clear the table and load the dishwasher after the kids are in bed—for extra pay, of course.

NANNIES AND AU PAIRS

Nannies

Quick—think of a nanny and what comes to mind?

If you're like most people you might picture a terribly proper, no-nonsense, conservatively dressed British powerhouse who administers healthy doses of elixir as well as discipline—or even Mammy from *Gone With the Wind*. Few nannies resemble either. Today they are more likely to be young (or young-at-heart), educated and in demand.

By definition, a nanny is someone whose primary responsibility is the care and development of children. Housework is usually not included in the job description.

Nannies can live in or out. Some nannies are self-professed while others are graduates from accredited nanny schools, completing extensive training in child development, child psychology, health, safety and first aid, creative play, children's nutrition, infant care and employer/employee relations.

How to Find a Nanny

There are several ways to acquire a nanny. You can advertise in the newspaper, but be prepared for impostors as well as the real thing. Or you can go through a nanny agency (check in the yellow pages under "Child Care" as well as "Employment Agencies") and pay a fee from 50 to 100% of the nanny's first month's salary. Check out as many nanny agencies as possible before making a decision because services vary.

Begin by calling the agencies to request written information about their service. How did they sound over the phone? Did they seem helpful and genuinely interested in answering your questions? Sometimes agencies are busy when you call. If that's the case, did they offer to call you back at a later time to avoid rushing your questions, or did they try to get off the phone as soon as possible?

Once you've reviewed the brochures, it's time to visit the offices. Unless there's a real shortage of agencies, try to interview at least two agencies before deciding to go with your favorite. Some people even register with more than one agency to increase their chances of getting a wide pool of nannies to choose from. Plan on at least an hour to discuss your questions and concerns. Ask for references of people with successful placements, and call them when you get home. Also, don't forget to ask about provisions if the nanny doesn't work out within a certain time period as well as for information about screening and placement standards. Ask to see an employment application to learn what kind of questions they ask applicants. How long has the agency been in business? Call the Better Business Bureau and Department of Consumer Affairs to uncover any past or current problems.

One advantage of using a nanny agency is the convenience of letting someone else do the groundwork based on your specific needs and expectations. You conduct the final interviews and make the selection. There is usually a trial period during which time both sides evaluate chances for success. In most cases, if things don't work out the nanny is replaced by the agency. You can save lots of time and energy by using a reputable nanny agency.

What about employment agencies that handle nanny placements? Use the same screening and evaluation procedure with employment agencies as with nanny agencies, and you may find the ideal nanny.

Obviously, nanny schools are a valuable resource for parents seeking qualified nannies. The sooner you explore this option, the better, since most schools have a long waiting list for their graduates. Many people get on the list as soon as they find out about the pregnancy. Graduates are in demand because they are carefully screened and complete a comprehensive training program which many parents feel makes them more committed than the average person. Some parents even offer a scholarship to guarantee access to a graduate.

This may seem like a lot of work but the advantages of doing your homework in the beginning of a search saves having to repeat the process over again later because of a hasty decision or poor research. I promise—it's worth it. Not only will you make good decisions but you will have peace of mind knowing you explored all logical options before concentrating on what was right for you and your family.

Check your local yellow pages under "schools" and "child care" for nanny colleges in your area but also be sure to call the Better Business Bureau, Department of Consumer Affairs and local licensing agency, if applicable, to check on complaints.

Au Pairs

The term "au pair" means "on par" or "equal." According to the American Institute of Foreign Study, a legal au pair is a person who has contracted to come to this country for a specific period of time (12 months). In exchange for a cultural experience, they assist the host family with child care for up to nine hours a day five and one-half days a week. Typical duties include activities such as feeding, bathing and playing with the children and responsibilities such as supervising the children at play or while they watch TV and being present when the parents are not at home. Parents obtain legal au pairs through foundations such as the American Institute for Foreign Study. Fees are paid to the foundation by the host family, not the au pair. In addition to the foundation fees, the host family also pays transportation costs (round trip) and approximately $100 per week for pocket money while the au pair is living in their home.

It takes two to three months from the application process to the arrival of the au pair, so the sooner you begin, the better. Most au pairs arrive during the summer months.

The advantages to this type of arrangement are quite unique. According to the American Institute of Foreign Study's *Au Pair in America:*

> The Foundation believes that everyone benefits from this exchange. The Host Family enjoys the company and intercultural richness of the Au Pair. The children enjoy the consistent companionship and support of a single care giver. The Au Pair enjoys the opportunity to see America from an ideal vantage point, the American family. The foundation provides a safety net on on-going involvement in the match to assure that problems are resolved and that no one is exploited. In the case of mis-matches or when problems are irreconcilable, alternate placement will be attempted as quickly as possible.

For more information on this valuable service, call or write the foundation. In addition to several brochures, it will also send a host family application.

It may be just what you've been looking for!

> Au Pair in America
> 102 Greenwich Avenue
> Greenwich, Connecticut 06830
> 203-869-9090

Some Final Thoughts

There are many advantages to being an in-home provider. Students can do homework during baby's nap, meals are provided, and flexibility is built into the job (how many jobs allow you to take a walk outside when you need some fresh air?). The most important aspect of being an in-home provider is the opportunity to have a positive impact on the life of another human being. What could be more important?

It's a two-way street. I've stressed treating your provider like a professional, but don't forget to also treat her like a member of the family. In addition to paying on time, calling when you'll be late and stocking the house with food for each day, you can recognize the importance of her role in the life of your child by giving praise and encouragement. With a little practice, you *can* have a business relationship and a personal relationship. The key is trust and communication.

5

FAMILY DAY CARE HOMES

Family day care homes are one of the oldest forms of child care. A family day care home can be described as child care provided in a home other than the child's. It can be done on a small informal basis (as my mom watching little Freddy from down the street), a large-scale operation with up to 12 children in a licensed home with paid helpers, or anything in between.

Family day care homes differ from babysitting in that a babysitter provides care, usually in your home, for a limited number of hours on a sporadic basis and is chosen from a pool of babysitters you use. Someone who provides regular care for a set number of hours can have a tremendous influence on the development of your child, not to mention your own peace of mind.

In California, for example, there are two types of licensed family day care homes: small family day care homes provide care for up to six children while large family day care homes provide care for up to 12 children. Any facility with over 12 children is considered to be a child care center and falls under different licensing regulations. Because regulations vary from state to state, check the regulations information in the Resources section to confirm the requirements in your state, or call your state Department of Social Services for up-to-the-minute information.

Advantages and Disadvantages

Why use a family day care home rather than a child care center? Many parents find the lower ratio of children to providers comforting and prefer a home setting to that of a center-based operation. Other advantages of using a family day care home include:

Siblings can stay together: Family day care homes are excellent for families with children of different ages. Everyone from the baby to the kids who need before- and after-school care can receive care and supervision from the same person in the same place.

51

Mildly ill child care: A family day care home is able to care for children when they wake up with the sniffles and you have a board meeting at 8:30. The provider will usually isolate your child from the others and keep a special eye on him throughout the day, much the same way you would if you were able to stay home.

A variety of birth order experiences: An only child can experience what it feels like to have to share. Also, imagine the fun of being the youngest one at home but being looked up to as a "big kid" at the family day care home by little ones. Even older kids benefit by exposure to a variety of children.

A stable environment during times of transition: A family day care home can provide the type of stability a child craves during times of great stress, such as divorce or separation. Even something as scary as kindergarten can be fun if the child has had a consistent family day care home and has learned about kindergarten via kids having gone through similar experiences.

Convenience: Parents can choose between a family day care home near their own home, place of employment or children's school.

Affordability: Generally speaking, family day care homes are less expensive than child care centers. This varies greatly depending on your area.

Kids get to be with their school friends: If you use a neighborhood family day care home, chances are the other kids will be attending the same school as your child. This can be especially helpful if the provider drops the kids off at school in the morning and picks them up again after school. Kids like the "club" sense that can develop when they share the same family day care home. I know of one provider who even had T-shirts printed that read, "I'm one of Sarah's Kids." After-school activities like Brownies and soccer can also be more manageable if several of the children participate.

A more informal structure: Sometimes children do better in a less structured, less populated environment. If your child is sensitive to crowds or noise, a family day care home can certainly offer an environment compatible with her needs. This is not to imply that only family day care homes can provide this type of environment—many child care centers, especially the smaller ones, have a low-key environment.

Field trips and learning experiences: Taking six children to the zoo is a lot easier to manage than taking 35 children or more. Depending on the skills and talents of the provider, a family day care home can offer regular learning experiences, such as cooking, planting a garden, caring for pets, and field trips with fewer complications. Again, this is not meant to imply that child care centers do not offer field trips or learning experiences! But because of sheer numbers alone, a family day care home may be able to fit these objectives into their program with greater frequency than some child care centers.

Evening, weekend or overnight care: Depending on the provider, you may be able to use your family day care home as a backup for evening, weekend or overnight care. This can be critical to parents who travel frequently in their careers.

These are only a few of the advantages parents recite when asked what they like about family day care homes.

But what about people who have had bad experiences with family day care homes? The following disadvantages also need to be considered.

Care is generally unsupervised: Under no circumstances should you consider placing your child in an unlicensed home if that option is available in your state. It's true that a license doesn't guarantee quality child care, but an unlicensed home makes a statement about the commitment on the part of the provider to adhere to minimum health and safety standards. Even in a licensed home, the provider is unsupervised for the duration of your child's stay with the exception of parents coming to drop off or pick up their children. Short of installing closed circuit TV cameras in every room of the house, parents must rely on their intuition and the responses of their children to know whether or not abuse is occurring.

Family day care homes do not require minimum educational standards for providers: Many child care centers do. While a degree in child development is not necessary to provide a safe, stimulating and loving environment, it is certainly something to consider when choosing child care.

Family day care homes may go out of business with little or no warning: Staff changes in a child care center do not disrupt the overall operation of the center. Also, some family day care home providers stay open on school days only, leaving the parents in a lurch during holidays, teacher work days and the provider's vacation.

If you are considering using a family day care home, a good place to begin is in the yellow pages under "Child Care—Resource and Referral." Many cities have state-funded agencies established to provide free resource and referral services to parents seeking child care. They will give you names and phone numbers of child care centers and family day care homes by zip code.

Registration

As mentioned earlier, states vary in their requirements for the operation of a family day care home. For example, in some states registration is voluntary or nonexistent while in others it is mandatory. Even the term registration is relative. Some states maintain only names and addresses of people operating a family day care home while others perform background checks and inspections. Obviously, a uniform code of standards needs to be developed on a national level, but at this time each state sets its own standards (or nonstandards). The same can be said for licensing requirements.

Why a License?

A license does not automatically guarantee that a family day care home is good, but it's an excellent barometer of the provider's commitment to establishing and maintaining standards. If someone is *not* licensed, there is usually a good reason for it—the very least of which is lack of interest in the application procedure. In some states there is no application fee for a family day care home license. If someone in these states tells you they can't afford to be licensed, they are either unfamiliar with the procedure or are referring to improvements necessary for health and safety standards.

A licensing supervisor in one state stressed how supportive the licensing workers are with new people—these workers want and need more family day care homes and will do everything they can to ensure the success of a new operation. Licensing workers are an excellent resource for parents considering a family day care home, yet few people are aware that licensing workers—if their caseloads allow—will discuss various licensed family day care homes and even make referrals. These people have an advantage over resource and referral services in that they are the ones who are actually in the field and are familiar with the providers. This particular supervisor also suggested that parents continue to call the licensing office on a regular basis (every six months or so) to check on possible complaints.

Case Study: Getting a License in California

Licenses in California are issued for a period of three years with inspections being held prior to licensing and whenever complaints are reported. Also, only 10% of all licensed homes have unannounced inspections annually, so it's possible that a family day care home provider may not see another inspection for three years after initial licensing. Statistics are not available on the percentage of homes still in operation one year after licensing.

When someone applies for a license, the applicant must submit to background checks on himself as well as any other adults in the home. This check reveals criminal records as well as any activity with Children's Protective Services or other law enforcement agencies that investigate child abuse. If the applicant has been in the state less than two years, a fingerprint check is run through the FBI for similar information.

Next, an orientation is scheduled for an in-service training that includes health and safety standards. The applicant goes home with a checklist to aid in "kid-proofing" the home and an appointment with a licensing worker who will come to the home for an on-site inspection. In the meantime, a tuberculosis test is required before the license is issued.

Licensing also provides the applicant with certain paperwork that must be shared with the parents: an emergency information card, a medical release form, a sexual abuse pamphlet and an information sheet—both with receipts which must be signed by the parents—and an insurance waiver form which must also be signed by the parents if the provider does not carry liability insurance.

The license will either be for a small family day care home (six or fewer children, maximum three infants) or a large family day care home (seven to 12 children, maximum four infants). A large family day care home requires another adult worker in addition to the primary care provider. Any of the provider's children under 12 years old are included in the count. Applicants are advised of any family day care home provider associations and of resource and referral services with which to register as well as workshops, seminars and college classes that would improve or enhance their services.

The licensing worker is the link between the parents and the providers. They provide on-going information and support to the provider and act as a watchdog for the safety of the children involved, but they can't do their job without input from the parents.

QUESTIONS TO ASK YOURSELF AND THE PROVIDER

Does the provider meet my needs based on the answers to the Self Test?

Is the provider the kind of person *I* would want to spend the day around?

Is the house squeaky clean, or does it have that "kids live here" look about it?

Is the provider warm and loving with children, meeting their questions with a smile and eye contact on their level?

Are the hours of operation, including nonschool days and vacations, compatible with my schedule?

Who is the backup person when the provider is ill?

What is the provider's philosophy on child rearing?

Is a sample menu of snacks and meals available for review?

Does the provider have any child development training and/or experience in child care?

Is there a mix of physical activities and quiet activities?

Is the environment well-lighted and inviting, with child-scaled furniture and appropriate age-level toys?

What is the policy on discipline?

Does the provider keep a log for each child, recording minor problems that occurred during the day, injuries and treatments, cute things he/she said?

Is the personal area of the home distinct from the kid's area?

Is the outdoor area safe with enough room for the children to run and play freely?

Does the provider have pets? If so, will the pet roam freely or be tied when the children are there?

Does the provider seem to welcome parents—including surprise visits by them?

Has the provider had first aid training, including CPR, within the past two years, and if not, would she be willing to take classes?

Are individual needs of children considered during nap time, or must all children be on the same schedule?

How much TV is allowed and when?

Are field trips included on a regular basis to places such as the park, grocery store or zoo?

Does the provider seem up-to-date on current child development theories or willing to try new methods of coping with difficult behavior?

Is the provider willing to share names and phone numbers of current parents as well as past parents who have used the family day care home?

What are the provider's feelings about toilet training?

The list goes on and on. Hopefully, the answers to these questions, as well as any not listed that are important to you, will enable you to evaluate a potential family day care home.

WHAT TO WATCH OUT FOR

NO LICENSE (if applicable).

Parents are discouraged from dropping-in unannounced.

The provider accepts the children and delivers them only through the front door—parents are not allowed inside.

You have a personality conflict with the provider either on the phone or in person.

The house is not childproof—breakables and unsafe or inappropriate furnishings are in the children's area.

There are too many children or too great age differences making supervision difficult.

The provider seems short and irritable with the children.

There is an unusually heavy emphasis on money.

Your questions are met with hostility or indifference.

Unresolved complaints have been filed with the licensing agency.

There are not enough toys for all the children.

The kids seem bored and restless.

The TV is on the entire time you are there (unless it's something like *Sesame Street*).

You have a nagging feeling that something is just not right.

What Next?

Try to arrange at least two visits before you make a decision. The first visit should *not* include your child. This will enable you to observe without distractions. You know your child well enough to evaluate if she would initially fit into the group. This first visit should be scheduled with a set amount of time in mind for observation, but with some flexibility in case a longer stay is appropriate. Ideally, you should stay long enough to have your questions answered and still be able to observe the provider in action with the children.

If you like what you see during the first visit, go home and call the references (see Sample Questions for References, page 38) before you set up a second visit. During the second visit, bring your child along and allow her to interact *if she wants to* with the other children. Some kids will feel better sticking close to Mom until they get comfortable. This is a good time to observe the provider with your child: Does the provider allow the child to proceed at her own pace, encourage her to join the group or ignore him altogether? Stay in the background, if at all possible, and watch your child with the other children.

At this point, you will have a pretty good idea about whether or not this is going to work. If you still have doubts, simply state that you need to think about it a while longer.

Don't make a decision in haste because the provider is pressuring you—good providers respect your thoroughness and concern. If your instincts say this would be a loving, stimulating place for your child and your child doesn't want to leave when it's time to go home, by all means sign her up! But your job's not over yet. In fact, as we see again and again, it's never over.

Day Care, Guilt and Parenting:
A Family Day Care Provider Speaks Out

Tina Stewart is a 26-year-old family day care provider with a bachelor's degree in child development and plans for a master's degree in a related field. She opened her "Infants Only" family day care home a little over a year ago because of the rising need for this type of facility and her own preference for babies based on five years experience in a variety of child care centers and family day care homes. Tina is a home owner in a small neighborhood conveniently located near downtown Sacramento, California, making it easy for parents to transport their children before and after work. Her home has a cozy country look with the dining room converted to a day room for the babies' play area and with safety gates blocking access to the rest of the house. She has four babies, ages three months, four months, five and one-half months and 14 months. We talked one morning while the sun was shining through the playroom window and Austin, Tina's newest and youngest charge, cooed contentedly on the padded rug in the middle of the floor.

Q: What made you decide to go into this field?

T: I've always loved children, especially babies. That's why I studied child development in school. I had the opportunity to work in different child care settings—mostly child care centers—although I worked in a large family day care home for 12 children, too. When it came time to decide which direction to take, it didn't take much to realize I wanted more control than was possible in a child care center.

Q: What do you mean by "more control"?

T: Less structure and more time to give individual attention to kids. I strongly believe that infants need a lot of one-on-one interaction and sensory stimulus. I'm licensed for four babies but usually only have two or three at a time because of their parents' schedules. There's also a high turnover rate and poor pay in a center-based facility. I liked the idea of working out of my own home.

Q: Based on your experience, what kind of kids do best in a child care center?

T: Definitely kids over the age of two. I wouldn't hesitate sending my own children to a carefully researched child care center once they were old enough (Tina has no children of her own yet).

Q: Can you describe the typical parent that calls for information about your infant center?

T: They're almost all first-time parents returning to work after the birth of their child. I'm amazed that people wait until after their baby is born before they start checking things out. I would recommend visiting different places right after finding out about the pregnancy! That way, by the time you need to make a decision, you're already an expert. Plus, many places have a waiting list, and if you get on during the pregnancy, you have a better shot at an open slot after the baby is born.

Q: What kinds of questions do parents ask?

T: Their first questions over the telephone pertain to my hours and rates. If we get a good mutual feeling about each other, we usually arrange a visit as soon as possible. Surprisingly, few parents have questions when they come for a visit. The only thing they all want to know is what I do when the babies all cry at once.

Q: What do you do?

T: It rarely happens that they all need something at once. I keep a day chart (see sample) on each baby, so I pretty much know the last time they ate, slept, had a bowel movement, etc. Most of them have been here long enough that I can tell by the cry what they need.

Q: Just like a real mom?

T: I do feel like their real mom when they're with me, but I never lose sight of the fact that I'm part of the team, an important part, but not their real mother.

Q: What happens if nothing works?

T: I'm sure every parent can relate to that feeling of frustration when nothing seems to calm their babies down—especially the very young babies. Sometimes babies just need to cry for a while—just like at home. That's why it's so important to communicate with the parent about how the baby's day has been. If the baby has been doing a lot of crying at my house and it doesn't let up when they get home, then there's a problem that needs more attention than the baby who cries for an hour every night at about the same time.

Q: What are some benefits to using a family day care home for an infant?

T: Babies learn to entertain themselves as opposed to having someone pick them up the minute they start to cry. I have one mother who literally cannot stand to watch her child struggle. Chandra (the 14 month old) was stuck behind a pillow once and started whining. I said, "Come on, honey, you can do it!" and she got unstuck in less than a minute. You should have seen the satisfied look on her face. If her mom had been here, her mom would have rushed to help without giving Chandra a chance to try for herself.

Probably the top problems I see that face parents who work outside the home are guilt and overcompensation. They feel that since they haven't seen the baby all day they want to do more to make up for their absence. Honestly, babies love their moms and dads whether they see them all day long or just a few hours in the evening—there is nothing to make up. Maybe older kids feel the difference a little more, but babies are just happy people who pretty much accept what's going on as long as mom is happy to see them and conveys a feeling of confidence. That's more important than how many hours they spend together.

Q: What advice do you have for parents who are considering this type of care for their infant?

T: As I mentioned before, start looking as soon as you find out you're pregnant. Ask for references and call other parents who are currently using that family day care home as well as parents who have used it in the past. Ask those parents if their baby seems happy most of the time.

The biggest determination of success or failure, in my opinion, is the amount of communication that goes on before the baby is placed. Tell the provider your views on feeding—don't simmer quietly because you don't know how to contradict the provider—it's your baby! Be a fierce consumer when it comes to the care of your child. Call the licensing agency to see if anyone has filed a complaint against that provider, ask to see the license and be prepared to spend some time in the home to get a feel for the place. If you do only one thing, be sure to check references, even if you are uncomfortable about checking up on somebody.

Q: What are some things parents can do to maintain a good working relationship with the provider once their children are placed?

T: Common sense things like calling when they'll be late and paying on time. Even though I work out of my home, I still depend on a fixed income, so when someone wants to pay me "next time," it really throws things off. I work from 7:00 A.M. to 6:00 P.M. every day in a very physically demanding field. It would be nice if more parents gave me an occasional pat on the back about the job I'm doing. Some of them don't even like to go over their baby's day with me when they pick them up at night. They run in, grab them and want to run out. That's another reason I have a chart on all the babies. In case we don't get to talk, the parents can at least see what the day's been like for their babies when they sign out.

Q: Do you have any other suggestions for how parents can maintain a healthy relationship with a provider?

T: Just to remember that we're people, too. My dad died recently, and only two of the parents acknowledged it. That kind of hurt. I always thought the ultimate compliment from a parent would be a card on Mother's Day, but I'm not sure that's realistic. It's hard to know the balance between a work relationship and a friendship. I tend to see us as a team working for the best of all worlds for the baby. As long as we're daydreaming, I wish the parents could take turns spending just one day in my shoes to appreciate the amount of energy I put into their children. I love what I do, especially seeing the babies develop a strong sense of self-esteem, but this job comes with long hours, isolation and tremendous responsibility.

Q: Any last words of advice?

T: Just an observation really. I've noticed that mothers do best with part-time care. There's less guilt, and it gives them a chance to recharge. Babies, however, adjust better to a full-time schedule. If they're only here three or four hours, it's much more disruptive to their routine than spending the day here. They get used to being here in no time at all. It's the moms who have a hard time adjusting to full-time care. There's way too much guilt in the world.

Sample Day Chart—"Infants Only"

Name _____ Date _____

To be filled in by the parent:

Time In _____ Signature: _____

Time Out _____ Signature: _____

Ate Last: What? _____ When? _____

Slept Last: _____

Remarks: _____

_____

Health Check:

Initials (Parent & Caregiver): _____

To be filled in by the Caregiver:

Diapering: Time and Appearance

_____

_____

_____

Feeding: Time, What, How Much

_____

_____

_____

Naps: When, How Long

_____

_____

_____

Remarks:

_____

_____

_____

BIBLIOGRAPHY

Harms, Thelma. "Finding Good Child Care." *Parents,* August 1986.

Scarv, Sandra. *Mother Care, Other Care.* New York: Basic Books, 1984.

Squibb, Betsy. *Family Day Care and How to Provide It in Your Home.* Boston: The Harvard Common Press, 1980.

Wayman, Anne. *Successful Single Parenting.* Deephaven, Minn.: Meadowbrook Press (Simon & Schuster, dist.), 1987.

6

CHILD CARE CENTERS, NURSERY SCHOOLS AND PRESCHOOLS

Child care centers, nursery schools and preschools, like other forms of child care, should fulfill children's needs in five basic areas:

- ❖ Physical development
- ❖ Socialization skills
- ❖ Emotional needs
- ❖ Intellectual: Preparation for the future
- ❖ Freedom to express the sheer joy of childhood

Children need food, rest and exercise; contact with other children in a sensory-rich environment; approval and encouragement from the people in their lives; skills that will prepare them for the next step of their development (knowing the names of colors, simple counting, and so forth); and the undeniable pleasure of being a kid.

What do you picture when you think of child care centers? Sunny, happy places with giggling children interacting in constant harmony or dark, dreary places where hollow-eyed infants stare at blank ceilings while scowling, uniformed employees provide only the barest of custodial duties? Most of us fall somewhere in between these two extremes depending on our experience or lack of experience with child care centers.

The definition of a child care center also depends on which state you happen to live in. For example, in Texas a child care center is defined as ". . . a facility that provides care for less than 24 hours a day for more than 12 children under the age 14," while in Florida the definition of a child care centers is "(a facility which) serves groups of six or more children . . . utilizing subgroupings on the basis of age and special need but provides opportunity for experience and learning that accompanies a mixing of ages . . ." Whew!

In California a child care center is defined as a facility that provides care for 13 or more children and/or infants in less than a 24-hour period per day. A state agency handles licensing, complaints and inspections in a cooperative effort with the state fire marshal's office. The ratios of teachers to children are strictly enforced:

1:4   Infant center (under age 2)
1:12 Ages 2–5
1:15 School-age children

In general, educational requirements for teachers and aides in a publicly funded child care center versus a privately funded child care center are more stringent. This can range from concurrent enrollment in early childhood classes to a bachelor's degree, depending on the center.

The best way to become an expert on child care centers is to visit as many as possible, as soon as possible, before you feel pressured to make a decision.

There are many different kinds of child care centers. Some may have an emphasis on social interaction or play groups while others lean more towards an academic bent. For the sake of our discussion in this chapter, let's define an ideal child care center in general terms as:

a public or private facility meeting the needs of the children it serves by providing quality care that promotes self-esteem, provides stimulating activities relative to the child's development, promotes social interaction, is safe and (is) emotionally secure.

Again, for the sake of discussion, let's assume a child care center has more than 12 children with an age range from three to 12 years old.

Advantages and Disadvantages

Advantages to using a child care center include predictable hours and staff; lots of supervision and public scrutiny (parents come and go, tours are given, staff changes occur with the shifts); a structured environment similar to a school environment that helps prepare children for kindergarten; interaction with children of your child's own age and development; a variety of indoor and outdoor experiences, including field trips; and finally, the convenience of the center being located near your home or office. Many centers operate before- and after-school programs that include pickup and delivery to the school site.

Some child care centers even make it possible to observe your child in the center from your office through the use of the Internet. A small camera is mounted in the room and records live action. Parents can get a still picture of their child's classroom every 30 seconds. If your center offers this option, all you need is a modem and the daily security code to block out curious net surfers.

Disadvantages include high turnover for teachers and staff; exposure to more childhood illnesses through close contact with a variety of other children; and a "busy" environment that may not be appropriate for children who are especially sensitive to noise and crowds. Depending on your area, cost may be a disadvantage, as child care centers are generally more expensive than other forms of child care.

Resources: Where and How to Begin Looking

Unless you have collected a list of child care centers to visit from word-of-mouth referrals, the best place to begin looking for one is the yellow pages of the telephone directory under "Child Care—Resource and Referral."

A resource and referral service (R&R) is an organization with access to information about child care in your specified area or zip code. Some people want child care near their home while others prefer a location on their way to or near their office.

As a result of the growing demand for quality child care, a new service has been created—the personal or private resource and referral service. For a fee, usually around $25, you can get information on the types of child care available that meet your specific needs. This service will even call for you to see if a particular center has any openings.

This is great if you are short on time, resources and confidence.It does raise a few questions, though.

For example, why would you pay for a service that is offered for free through public R&R agencies? The private agency can provide information about basic services, but you still need to personally visit a site before you decide, so why not do it all yourself? And just because they verify an opening on the day that they call is no guarantee that it will still be available by the time you follow up. Lastly, and most importantly, the more exposure you have to child care options, the better you will feel about your final decision. It will be an educated choice rather than a choice made in haste.

A good private R&R service will provide services such as educating you about free child care resource and referral services, asking extensive questions to ensure adequate research on their part, and offering non-traditional options which might include flex-time or combined child care (an in-home person during the morning who would then drop off your child at her nursery school for the afternoon).

A private R&R service is a great option for employers who want to offer their employees concrete help with their child care dilemma. More about that is discussed in the chapter on employer-sponsored child care.

If you can't find a listing for a resource and referral service in the yellow pages, try looking in the white or blue pages under "State of _____, Licensing" for the regulatory agency in your state. This office will know who to call for information or will provide that information themselves, depending on their workload. After all, these are the folks who issue licenses after inspections, so they have a pretty good handle on what's out there. Also, check the appendix of this book for ideas.

Sometimes you may not be able to get through to the licensing agency because the telephone lines are busy. If this is the case, dig out your clipboard, paper and pencil, and go back to the yellow pages.

Begin by skipping the alphabetized listing of child care centers and go directly to the ads. You'll be using the alphabetized ads as a last resort because, unfortunately, they aren't arranged geographically. Unless you live in a small town, there will be a large number of listings for child care centers.

Don't be swayed (one way or the other) by slick full-page ads. Many good centers don't have an advertising budget, nor do all centers with an advertising budget reflect cold impersonal service. The ads will merely screen centers based on your preference regarding location and basic philosophy: They're a time saver.

Once you've got 10 child care centers (or, if you live in a small town, a minimum of three) that fall within the geographical boundaries you've set and also sound like nice places to be, you're ready to gather some information over the phone.

Keep your priorities in mind: Do you want to start with a morning program and work your way up to full-time care? Is it important that your child be in a structured environment, or do you prefer a less-structured center with lots of time for free play? Other basic information to ask will include such things as fees; hours of operation; types of programs available (part-time, full-time, computers, gymnastics); are meals included; how many children attend and ages; ratio of staff to children; special considerations (must children already be toilet trained); and basic philosophy of the center. I know the basic philosophy question can be a tough one to ask because it's vague (on purpose), but believe me, centers are used to answering it!

Refer to sample questions in the previous chapters as well as your responses on the Self Test to help you narrow down your needs and expectations.

Armed with this information and a clipboard full of questions, you're ready to make that first call. Try not to call early in the morning when kids are arriving or during lunch. If the person on the phone sounds hurried but polite, ask if there is a better time for you to call back. That kind of consideration is really appreciated.

Besides basic information, you may also be curious about the following additional information: Who is the owner? Who is the director?

What is the turnover rate for teachers, aides and directors? Who takes over when the director leaves the site? What supplies does the center provide, and what supplies must the parent provide? At what point are parents called if there is a problem? Is a job description available for the aides as well as the teachers? What type of educational requirements do the teachers have to fulfill? How long has the center been in business?

This is only the information-gathering portion of your search. You'll be asking many more questions during the site visit. Right now you're just trying to get a general idea of what's available, so you can compare and contrast the options.

Review the list after you've called all 10 centers, and decide on three or four you'd like to learn more about through a site visit. Call those centers back to arrange an appointment with the director.

Do not drop in on them for an initial visit because you need to do more than just poke your head in—it takes time to really get a feel for a place. Some parents like to bring their child with them for the initial visit while others like to reserve that for a second visit. You and your child's temperament will guide you on that issue.

You are now ready for your first site visit. But before you walk through the door, take the time to (again) review the results of the Self Test and refresh your memory about your priorities. And don't forget your clipboard. (Don't worry; you won't look strange. Every teacher and director I've ever spoken to has made it a point to stress how few parents are prepared when they come for a visit. They'll be impressed that you care enough to do your homework.)

Draw up a list of questions based on your own brainstorming to add to the lists of sample questions that follow. Choose the ones you'd like to have answered, and write them down so you won't forget. Treat this as you would a business transaction by being alert and prepared. But don't turn off your instincts—they're your most valuable tool.

WHAT TO LOOK FOR IN A GOOD CHILD CARE CENTER

Physical Characteristics

1. Are there lots of things to climb on and crawl through?
2. Is the outside play area safe with a variety of textures to play with/on (grass, pavement, sand)?
3. Where do tired kids lie down?
4. Does each child have his own storage area with his name on it for drawings, announcements, personal items?

5. Are there quiet places and rowdy places? Games? Child-sized furniture and plumbing fixtures?
6. Are there lots of books, art supplies and specific activity areas, such as a housekeeping center, a building center?
7. Inspect the bathrooms, but don't be surprised if they fail the white glove test. Notice whether they are just messy or really dirty. Ask how often they are cleaned and whether a janitorial service or staff person is used for this responsibility. Do all children share the same bathroom, or are there separate facilities for boys and girls?
8. Is the license prominently displayed? When was the last inspection? Call the appropriate regulatory agency (information can be gained by examining the license) to see if any complaints have been registered against the center.
9. Make a note of the mileage to the center and how long it takes to get there. Will traffic patterns differ during the hours you would be using the center?
10. Ask about the center's policy on the prevention of disease and accidents. Are teachers and aides trained in first aid? Have they had any major illness or accidents in the last two years?
11. Are there lots of windows (with safety glass) to enable the children to observe nature as well as the comings and goings of adults?
12. Are gate latches high enough to be out of reach of little fingers?
13. Is there enough inside and outside room for each child?
14. Is there a supervised isolation area for sick children waiting to be picked up by their parents?
15. Is this the kind of place where I would enjoy spending time? Can I imagine my child there?
16. Ask for a sample schedule of the day; meal/snack menu; a brochure, if they have one; and paperwork necessary for enrollment. (This is good to have whether you choose that center or not. It will give you an idea of its thoroughness and expectations.)
17. Is toilet training included? What method is used?
18. How are parents involved with the center? Is participation encouraged or interpreted as interference? (For example, what if you wanted to have lunch with your child at the center?)
19. Does the center have a doctor on call? When are emergency procedures followed (only for broken bones? high fever?)?
20. What is the policy for your child's sick leave and vacation? Is the center closed on certain holidays and open on others? Is the center open on days when school is closed, such as teacher work days? Does it have a summer program?

21. If exploring the center for after-school care, does the center provide transportation to and from school? Are there age-appropriate activities for school-age kids apart from the preschool kids?
22. Ask for references, preferably from parents with children already enrolled in the center.

Psychological Characteristics

1. Is it bright and cheery with kids' artwork displayed on the walls, bulletin boards with various themes and a generally good atmosphere to it?
2. Are you greeted warmly by a receptionist, director or teacher? Take advantage of any time spent waiting in the lobby to observe group interaction, if possible.
3. Do the kids seem happy?
4. Are hugs given freely and often?
5. When teachers speak to a child, is it at the child's eye level? This may be an unfair observation because all that bending could be stressful to a healthy back. Still, I can't help but be impressed with teachers who consistently relate to kids at their own level.
6. What method of discipline is used, and how does it change with various age groups?
7. Does the center allow a transitional object, such as a blanket or teddy, until the child feels comfortable with her new surroundings?
8. What if my child was tired but it wasn't nap time yet? Or, what if my child was not tired during nap time? Are quiet activities available apart from the group?
9. Can children request seconds or thirds of snacks or lunches?
10. Do I feel hurried through the tour, or does the director invite me to sit in on story hour or observe on my own without her being there for part of the tour?

Making Your Decision

You get the idea. Ask anything that's on your mind and stay as long as it takes to get a feel for the center.

Even if you're absolutely convinced that this is the ideal place for your child, don't make any decisions until you've had a chance to see other places and definitely not until your child has had a chance to preview the center. Good center directors will encourage you to shop around and may even provide you with a list of other centers in the area. This is a good sign.

IF YOU'RE NOT COMFORTABLE WITH *ANY* OF THE CENTERS YOU VISITED, KEEP TRYING UNTIL YOU FIND ONE THAT MEETS YOUR REQUIREMENTS. Or reconsider the decision for this type of child care. Remember, the answer is within you about what's right for your child and what's right for you. It only works if everyone is happy—parents as well as children.

Don't settle just because you feel discouraged. Trust me, it's better to put the time in now and find a place that really suits your needs and those of your child than to have to make a change six months down the road.

The search for a child care center can be especially time-consuming if you're employed outside the home. But you take time off for a dental or medical appointment, right? Take the same time off to visit child care centers or go during your lunch hour, before work or after work. Remember, though, these can be very busy times at child care centers. You may not get as full a picture as you would during other times, but at least you'll have physically visited the center. After all, your child will be spending a lot of time there. It's important to thoroughly research your options.

If your employer is not supportive, give her the benefit of a doubt—approach her and ask for time off to search for quality child care arrangements, offering to put in extra hours or do extra work at home if necessary. Or you might consider enlightening her about the corporate benefits of addressing child care (see chapter 9). If necessary, begin researching companies that have a better family policy.

Remember, the time you take in the beginning will be well worth the peace of mind you feel after an informed, well-researched decision.

MONTESSORI SCHOOLS

Dr. Maria Montessori (1870–1952) was the first woman to be trained and licensed as a physician in Italy. Subsequently, she became concerned about the education of young children. After carefully observing children and recording their behaviors, needs and interests, she developed a method of teaching which has greatly influenced educational practice during the past 80 years. Dr. Montessori based this method on a child-centered approach. She encouraged sequential learning in a pre-pared environment in which children progress at their own rates and according to their own interests. Her designs for teaching apparatus have proven to be invaluable.

Dr. Montessori believed children learn best by doing. She wrote:

The secret of good teaching is to regard the child's intelligence as a fertile field in which seeds may be sown to grow under the heat of flaming imagination. Our aim therefore is not merely to make the child understand, and still less to force him to memorize, but so to touch his imagination as to enthuse him to his most innermost core. We do not want complacent pupils, but eager ones: we seek to sow life in the child rather than theories, to help him in his growth, mental and emotional as well as physical, and for that we must offer grand and lofty ideas to the human mind, which we find ever ready to receive them, demanding more and more.

The Montessori method is an approach to education which emphasizes the potential of the young child. This method develops each child's potential by means of a beautifully prepared environment, utilizing Montessori-trained teachers and scientifically developed learning materials and activities. Montessori schools originated in 1908 and have been going strong ever since.

The purpose of Montessori schools is to help students to develop a love of learning! Working in specially prepared classrooms enables students to develop the prime elements of character, freedom, concentration, independence and cooperation, while absorbing the academic concepts which they will need in higher education.

The qualities and skills that students learn may be applied everywhere. Montessori is a preparation for life. Learning to concentrate, to stay on task and to problem solve are components of the thinking process that are essential to all learning, regardless of where this learning takes place. In addition to developing excellent study skills, students are nurtured in an environment designed to enhance their self-esteem.

Montessori schools believe that:

- Children function best under conditions of trust, support, encouragement and success.
- Learning should be an active process.
- Children develop at different rates and have different strengths and weaknesses.
- Children should learn to function as cooperative members of a group.
- Children learn best when they are interested in the subject.
- Children should learn how to learn and how to make good decisions.

This information is gratefully adapted with permission of the Village Montessori School in Sacramento, California, with special thanks to its director, Karen Lecy.

HEAD START

In 1964, the Economic Opportunity Act was established to combat the effects of poverty. It began in 1965 by enrolling 550,000 students in 2,500 child development centers. To date, almost 10,000,000 children have been served.

The philosophy behind Head Start is to help children achieve a positive outlook on life through success in school and daily activities by improving the child's health; encouraging self-confidence, spontaneity, curiosity and self-discipline; and enhancing the child's mental processes and skills. The program also promotes a sense of dignity and self-worth for the child and the child's family. By supporting the relationships within the family and by creating confidence in the child's ability to deal with the present as well as the future, patterns and expectations for success become realistic expectations.

Longitudinal studies, specifically the Lazar study, found that children from Head Start programs did better than children of poverty that did not attend Head Start. They were found to be more strongly committed to school success and displayed less frequent deviant behavior. Early intervention does produce results.

Head Start programs can be center-based or even home-based, predominantly serving the needs of children from three to six years old, although services for low-income families with children below one to three years old are available in some parts of the country.

The components of Head Start include:

❖ Education
❖ Parent involvement
❖ Service to handicapped children
❖ Health services (medical, dental, early screening & follow-up)
❖ Social services
❖ Nutrition
❖ Staff development

Children in poverty are not the only ones eligible for Head Start. About 10% of Head Start enrollment must include children with special needs, such as handicapped children.

For more information about Head Start programs, contact the Head Start Bureau listed below or your local social service agency.

Head Start Bureau
Department of Health and Human Services
P.O. Box 1182
Washington, DC 20013

7
CHILD CARE ALTERNATIVES

Now that you've familiarized yourself with in-home care, family day care homes and child care centers, what if none of those options speak to your situation?

Maybe you only need occasional child care or an organized part-time program completely separate from full-time curriculum.

One mother I know had a hard time finding a program for her three-year-old because she was looking for a traditional nursery school that offered a program for only three hours per morning. There were many preschool programs to choose from but few that offered less than four-hour slots. By limiting her child's attendance, she also limited her child's participation in projects and disrupted the continuity of the preschool schedule. In other words, her child would be there for the beginning of a project but not necessarily for the end. Plus, the expense was the same whether her child attended nine, 15 or 20 hours a week. She experienced problems when exposing her child to other three-year-olds who had been in day care most of their lives and, in her opinion, were more aggressive than her child. The validity of her instincts regarding "career" day care children is discussed in chapter 11.

In any case, there *are* other options out there. Once you begin to explore these options, it will be easier to construct a personal child care plan which satisfies everyone.

The Resource Book

When I was looking for a roommate in college, I found help at the student housing office in the form of a resource book. I simply looked in the section under "Roommates Wanted" for a compatible match in an existing home or apartment. As my needs changed, I returned to the resource book and explored the options under "Homes for Rent" for my next residence. When that became too costly, I once again utilized the resource book, this time by filling out a card and filing the information under "Roommates Wanted" which prompted calls from potential roommates looking for a room in my house.

This same concept can be applied to child care.

The Resource Book is simply a way to match people who need occasional child care with people who want to provide that service in a place where both gather. This could be established at a church, gym, college campus, community center, tennis club, anywhere.

A simple three-ring binder can be used with two distinct sections: one for people who need child care; one for people who want to provide their services.

A natural place for a Resource Book would be in local child care centers. Everyone benefits—the parents who need occasional child care as well as teachers and aides who may want to earn extra money during their time off from work. Directors vary in their response to this suggestion. However, if you point out that you won't actually be stealing their employees, rather providing a way to enhance their income and experience, you will probably get a go-ahead.

Remember, the success of this approach depends on your ability to advertise its existence!

Posters and word-of-mouth are always good bets, especially if you are recruiting in a large facility, such as a church or community center. You may have to do the groundwork to get it rolling, but once the Resource Book is in place, it is fairly easy to maintain.

Child Care Co-ops

Child Care co-ops have been in existence for as long as there have been neighbors and friends who informally filled in for each other as needed. In spite of the fact that not all neighborhoods are filled with people who have young children or the time to exchange babysitting, co-ops have increased in popularity because of the benefits they provide in terms of convenience and affordability.

In a nutshell, a child care co-op is an arrangement in which families agree to provide child care for another family or families in exchange for reciprocal care when they need it. Sounds simple, doesn't it?

A co-op could be very informal, where the score is pretty even between two families who fill in for each other, or it can be highly structured with elaborate record keeping systems and rotating coordinators.

Advantages include the obvious savings in money. For example, I pay a sitter \$3–\$5/hour plus gas allowance and a tip every time I have a meeting, date or last-minute emergency. Dinner and the movies alone can amount to an extra \$20 in child care! And what about those days when teachers have an in-service obligation, giving the kids a day off, but you still have to work?

Child care is expensive!

A child care co-op can defray costs considerably and alleviate the usual guilt and complications of making the arrangements. After all, it's easier to call for child care knowing you have provided the same.

If you don't have a network already in place in your neighborhood, you could consider advertising in the classified ads of the newspaper but remember to be as specific as possible. This is especially true for defining geographic boundaries, ages of children and number of families.

You might try something like:

Wanted: 10 families to form child care co-op in the (zip code) area with children two to five years old. Save $$, meet your neighbors, introduce your kids to new friends! Call 555-0000 for more information.

An added bonus to child care co-ops is the community link you will develop with other parents like yourself. More than one friendship has developed out of the sense of camaraderie found in this situation.

Once you have 10 families (this is just an example, maybe a co-op of three will work for you, or 20) it's important to have an organizational meeting to establish guidelines. Again, this arrangement can be as formal or informal as the participants make it. The important thing to establish is a means of reciprocity so that one family won't be monopolizing the co-op, set down guidelines for health and safety, keep members informed and elect the first coordinator or secretary.

Reciprocity. Obviously, everyone has to do their share for the co-op to work, so a tracking system becomes necessary. A coupon system works well. Start each family with 10 hours of child care. Unless agreed upon ahead of time, no family should be issued more coupons until they have earned coupons by caring for someone else's child or children. If a family is running low on coupons, they can advise the secretary who will refer them first when people need child care. Be sure to divide the time coupons by half hours—that way time can be rounded to the nearest half hour.

Guidelines. Decide whether the co-op should be for day hours only or include evenings and weekends as well as whether child care should be in the provider's home or the child's home. Other issues would include having everyone fill out emergency information (see pages 42–43); rates for more than one child (1½ coupons per hour) and/or premium hour rates (1½ coupons per hour, per child for Saturday night); a policy regarding sick children; meals; transportation; whether or not the child is allowed to have friends visit; last-minute cancellation policy; and grace period for inactive members.

These are only suggestions to get you started. The relationships within the co-op will determine the guidelines with revisions as an expected part of the start-up process.

Paperwork. Someone has to keep track of members, distribute a monthly newsletter (optional) and be the liaison when problems occur.

Some co-ops elect a secretary paid with time coupons while others have a rotating system where families take turns being the secretary or coordinator.

If you are taking responsibility for organizing a new co-op, maybe you could be the secretary for the first month, keeping the following tips in mind:

1. Keep it simple. Maintain a current membership list of names, phone numbers, preferred times or days to care for children, ages and number of their own children, special restrictions or additional information. ("We have a big friendly dog that may frighten small children.")
2. Use a three-ring binder that can be easily transferred to the next rotating secretary. (Just to be on the safe side, make a Xerox copy in case that friendly dog mentioned above gets hungry.)
3. Have a form ready with spaces for the above information to be filled in by parents at the organizational meeting. Use an agenda at the organizational meeting to ensure covering the basics as well as leaving room for digression. Be specific on how long the meeting will last (from 6:00 to 7:30 P.M.) followed by a social hour afterwards—**you want to get business out of the way before getting to know each other better.**
4. Depending on the size of the co-op and the amount of discussion, a second meeting may be necessary before a charter is drawn up. A charter is simply a statement of the ground rules and a membership list.

I mentioned a monthly newsletter because this can be a great way to keep members informed regarding change of address, news about kids, an interesting book or article referral, notice of garage sales, a classified section for buyers and sellers—the list goes on. If your group has the time and the talent, by all means, give it a try!

In addition to a one-time buy-in, members should also pay a reasonable sum per year in membership dues to cover postage, with the balance being used toward an annual party with all the families getting together at the local park.

As you can see, there are many advantages to belonging to a child care co-op. A child care co-op may be something you'd like to explore even if your regular child care arrangements are elsewhere.

Parks, Recreation Departments and YMCAs

Traditionally, parks and recreation departments do not automatically spring to mind when you think about child care, but they can be exactly what you're looking for. Look in the white or blue pages under the city and county listings for information about which parks and recreation departments you live near, then call and ask it to send you a schedule of events and classes. Many YMCAs also offer a variety of children's activities.

The mother who had problems finding a three-hour preschool for her child was delighted to learn about a "Mom 'n' Me" parent participation program right in her neighborhood! Not only did her child have a play group experience, but Mom was able to go along and participate. Each parent took turns assisting the teacher during play time while the other parents met in a multipurpose room for coffee and discussion. It was a wonderful support system that also included speakers and child development films. Parents also took turns bringing a snack for the kids as well as for the other parents. (There was a mandatory "chocolate" clause in the parent group I belonged to: The parent's snack had to have chocolate in it at least twice a month!) The cost was much less than other programs, in part because of the parent participation. I still keep in touch with several of the moms I met during this time.

This can work well to enhance your regular child care situation. For example, suppose you'd had a wonderful in-home provider for your child since birth, but now the child shows signs of needing to be around other children. You don't need to eliminate in-home care; just add a good program from nine to noon on Monday, Wednesday and Friday. Your provider can be responsible for transportation to and from the program and even catch up on the laundry while your child is away!

If your community is fortunate enough to have a Boys and Girls Club, this is a good place to look for supervised activities, especially for older children. The membership cost is relatively low, and they are usually located near elementary schools. Visit several times at different times of the day to get a feel for the program.

School Districts

Just because your child is too young for kindergarten doesn't mean that your local school district doesn't have an appropriate program. Check in the white or blue pages for the country office of education, and call to see which school district you belong to as well as for advice on the variety of programs available. You will probably be surprised at the number of preschool options, some including parent participation.

The good news is that more and more schools are providing before- and after-school care for their students. The bad news is there aren't nearly enough—yet.

On-site before- and after-school care, also known as extended care, is the best of all worlds for many parents. Kids arrive after the parent has left for work and have the choice of eating breakfast, doing homework or just relaxing and playing with friends before school. When school gets out, there is usually a program that includes a snack, organized activity, homework time and lots of outdoor play. The parent comes by on the way home from work to pick up the child, and everyone is happy.

Your child's school may run an after-school program or it may contract out with a third party, such as Medallion School Partnerships (headquartered in Golden, Colorado), to administer the program. More and more schools use qualified outside vendors who specialize in school-age programs because it relieves the school district of liability and other administrative duties. The school provides the space in a multipurpose room or portable classroom and the vendor provides a turnkey after-school program, including staff and equipment. The program is funded by the parents who use it, and most have scholarships available for parents who qualify.

Another advantage to on-site extended care is the possibility for after-school activities. When my daughter was in an after-school program at her elementary school she was also on the school soccer team. The after-school program enabled her to check out for soccer practice and check back in afterwards. A note from parents is needed but most parents welcome the opportunity for their children to participate in sports without sacrificing safe supervision.

Since extended care usually involves a waiting list, see if your child can get on the waiting list the summer before her first year in school in order to receive priority registration in the fall.

Another valuable option offered by school districts is the availability of prekindergartens or transitional kindergartens. School readiness is a controversial issue with no clear-cut answers. If you feel, or have been advised, that your child may not be quite ready for kindergarten, one of these programs may be perfect. Transitional kindergarten or prekindergarten is generally more accelerated than preschool but not as accelerated as kindergarten.

Again, these are general guidelines. Each city, state, parent and child are different. Some of these programs may not be available in your area.

Relatives

Relatives are a great resource for families who have good lines of communication.

Advantages include the obvious bonding that will occur between your child and a close family member. If your mother is the one who will be caring for your child, you will already have been exposed to methods of reward and discipline. This may or may not be a source of comfort. Another advantage is the cost factor—often it will be minimal or nonexistent. Also, your chances of having a relative accept a sick child are probably better than with a nonrelative.

Disadvantages may range from power struggles over how to raise your child to resentment on the part of a provider/relative who feels taken advantage of.

The parents I've spoken with agree that it's more difficult to correct a family member than an employee. Also, the relationship between child and grandparent may change if they see each other on a daily basis rather than just at special times.

If you still have doubts, try it on a part-time basis in combination with a good part-time preschool.

Home-Based Businesses

Home-based businesses are fast becoming an acceptable way to balance work and home. You can be home with your child when needed and still have a career. Many colleges have community service programs that explore this topic in rich detail. If you've ever wondered if you've got what it takes to work at home, sign up for a class and find out. If you don't have access to a college in your area, check with the Better Business Bureau, Small Business Administration and Chamber of Commerce. They will probably have information to send you or know where to call to get it.

While you're patiently waiting to receive these brochures, sit down and take an inventory of your skills and interests to help narrow down the field a little. Sometimes it will be obvious. Maybe you were a whiz at word processing before the baby was born but just don't want to go back to an office. Or people are always asking for extra prints of the photographs you took of their kids at the soccer game. Do your dinner parties end with a standing ovation? Perhaps its time to convert that talent to dollars.

There is a *huge* demand for quality licensed child care providers. If this appeals to you, why not call the licensing agency and have them send you the information, or attend an orientation meeting? I've worked with parents who do all their homework and still can't decide on child care because all along the answer for them was *not* to put their child in child care! Becoming a provider enabled them to be with their children while expanding their home to include other children—to everyone's benefit.

Health Clubs

If you need child care only occasionally, as in three times a week while you go to the health club, ask other members what they do about child care if the club doesn't provide it. If everyone is having the same problem, why not get together and hire someone to watch the kids on an informal basis? The kids could be watched at the club, or you could rotate whose home is used. This works best on a buddy system with two people sharing one provider. You could alternate responsibility for finding a sitter on a monthly basis. Not only do you solve your child care problem, but you also reap the benefits of working out with a buddy—no more excuses.

Consider paying or booking your sitter in advance. I have a regular sitter on Monday nights for a class I'm taking and found that paying in advance creates a more businesslike arrangement with less of a chance for last minute cancellations. I know my sitter has blocked off four Monday evenings in September, and I don't have to worry about her being busy when I need her.

Yellow Pages

It's interesting to note the variety of listings in the yellow pages under "Child Care." You'll find information on professional organizations, child care centers, resource and referral services, care for the mildly ill child, respite care for children, drop-in child care and much, much more.

Word-of-Mouth

This cannot be stressed enough. If you literally ask everyone you have contact with, you will probably get some good referrals. Ask the referrals for referrals.

Keep your eyes open—child care providers are everywhere.

One of my best sitters came from a school auction. Meagan donated 15 hours of babysitting to my daughter's school which they in turn sold to the highest bidder. The money was then donated back to the school (You bet I bought it! A good sitter is worth double what I paid!) Not only did I gain a great sitter in Meagan, but she referred me to Tavia, Cindy and Lauren for those times when she was unavailable. In one fell swoop I gained four new people for my sitter list.

Another good resource is the grocery store. Did you ever notice how many young people work different shifts at the grocery store? I found out a lot of them were students who would love to earn some extra money, and since I'm one of those people who goes to the store almost every day, I felt as if I'd known them a long time.

If you use word-of-mouth consistently, you will get results!

Colleges

Speaking of students, I don't know too many that have all the money they need.

You can post notices around campus (get permission from the student activities office first) or ask the student employment office to post a job description for you.

Another advantage to using a college student is that you might find someone who is studying child development and will use the job as an extension of class. To interview early childhood or child development majors, contact the department head (the campus operator will know who that is) and tell them what you're looking for. Be sure to stress that you're seeking occasional as well as regular care. That way, if some students have schedules that conflict with your needs but would still like to care for your child in the evenings or on weekends occasionally, you'll have a backup list.

Don't forget to check with all types of colleges—state, community and private—in your area. Also call the director of the campus children's center.

The Red Cross

This is another well-kept secret. Did you know that many Red Cross chapters now offer Super Babysitter classes to certify babysitters? These classes include training in basic and emergency care as well as fun games to play with children.

Call your local Red Cross to see if such classes are offered in your area and to ask if you can distribute a flyer to the graduates with your name, telephone number, number and ages of kids and so forth. Some may even release the names and phone numbers of the graduates to the public, but this is rare. Or, better yet, be the first one to start a Resource Book at the local Red Cross chapter.

Churches and Synagogues

You don't necessarily have to be a member of a church or synagogue to take advantage of its child care services. Be sure to visit several different programs in your area before deciding on one, since many (but not all) programs have religious overtones. Different people are comfortable with different things, so it's important to know how much theology is involved before you enroll your child.

Don't automatically eliminate a church because of denomination. As in all forms of child care, base your analysis on personal observation and the program's ability to meet your needs and expectations.

Maintaining Your Babysitter Pool

Once you've found good sitters through a variety of resources, it's important to do a few simple things to ensure a happy relationship.

- Line sitters up as much in advance as possible.
- Discuss pay over the telephone, so you're in agreement from the beginning.
- Leave plenty of food and drinks in the house. Try to have the kids fed before the sitter gets there, or leave something to reheat for dinner. Don't expect a 14-year-old to prepare dinner from scratch unless that's been worked out in advance.
- Always, always, always leave a phone number where you can be reached and leave current emergency information posted in a prominent place.
- Call if you're going to be late. Don't say you'll be an hour late, then come home three hours late.
- Leave instructions on how to answer the telephone, whether it's okay to say you are out, what time you'll be back, etc.
- For an older child, don't use the term "babysitter," rather explain that Meagan will be over for a visit while Mom's gone but that Meagan will be in charge.
- If it's raining or stormy when you leave, be sure to locate a flashlight with live batteries in case of power failure, so the sitter won't have to rummage around in the dark.
- Recognize the sitter on special occasions such as birthdays and graduations.
- **Under no circumstances should you drive the sitter home after you've been drinking. Pay for a cab or let a designated driver take responsibility.**

If you follow these simple guidelines, the relationship between you and your provider will be a happy one. Show this list to your provider, and ask if there is anything that should be added.

BIBLIOGRAPHY

Henderson, Kathy. "The Saturday Night Solution." *Working Mother*, September 1989, 86–88.

8

THE CHILD CARE ACTION PLAN

Congratulations! You took the first step toward solving your child care dilemma when you picked up this book. That puts you way ahead of most people with the same problem because *you're doing something about it rather than just talking or worrying*. You've made a decision, a commitment.

The child care action plan is a process of breaking down the steps necessary to find good child care and deciding on a timetable to accomplish these goals. In other words, it's a blueprint.

You can either back into a plan by choosing a date to have child care in place (September 8), or you can evaluate how long each step will take and set a date based on these steps.

The following example of an action plan can be used as a guideline. Just modify it according to your needs and time constraints. Remember—*you* decide what's going to work for you, whether that takes three weeks or six months to accomplish.

Child Care Action Plan

	Dates
Finish reading this book	_____
Take the Self Test	_____
Develop a resource list of potential family day care homes or child care centers	_____
Make appointments with three family day care homes and child care centers in my area	_____
Conduct site visits and interviews	_____
Make unannounced site visit	_____
Make final visit with child	_____
Set start date, sign forms, submit paperwork	_____
Arrange trial period	_____

Conduct post-trial period evaluation   _____
Become involved, and stay on the alert   _____

By reading this book and completing the Self Test, you'll have a good idea of the type of care that is best for you to use. If you are choosing between a child care center and family day care home, as the action plan above indicates, your next step would be to sit down with a calendar and **realistically** fill in the dates to accomplish each step.

The reason I stress being realistic is because a plan can look great on paper, but will you realistically be able to interview three family day care homes and child care centers during the same week? If you overwhelm yourself, you may get discouraged and lose your ability to evaluate options effectively.

Developing an action plan for finding in-home care involves a few more steps, including: writing the ad, calling it in to the newspaper, a time period of screening calls, arranging personal interviews, checking references. Refer to the chapter 4 for more information.

For now, let's concentrate on the sample action plan. The majority of the steps involved in scheduling your action plan are self-explanatory. However, I want to stress the importance of scheduling a trial period while everyone is getting used to the new routine. Sometimes the provider will already have a time period established as the trial period, other times you may have to decide how long that should be. Two weeks to a month is usually average.

After the trial period, schedule a time on the calendar to sit down and review the events of the last few weeks with the caregiver. By scheduling an evaluation, you are assigning it a priority. By assigning it a priority, you are taking responsibility. By taking responsibility, you are relieving guilt and anxiety.

The last two items on the sample action plan are to get involved and stay alert. Many parents who work 40-plus hours per week feel guilty because they can't be there to cut out little bears with their child's class or to supervise a field trip. But you *can* donate the glitter for the little bear's vest or send along snack bags to be eaten on the field trip. Regardless of your child's age or your work schedule, there are things that you can do to stay involved. Check with the provider for suggestions, or come up with a few suggestions of your own.

I was fortunate when my daughter was in the second grade to be able to spend some time in her classroom every Monday afternoon. My heart sank when I first looked at the sign-up list for parental involvement because most tasks involved mornings when I would be in school. After talking to my daughter's teacher, we came up with a plan to have me come once a week for the last half hour of the day to read stories to the kids. Not only did I get to be a hero in my daughter's eyes because of the popularity of story hour, but I was able to incorporate requirements for my children's literature class in the process. They got stories; I got experience and college credit!

Not all arrangements are going to work out this well, but you get the idea. Do you have a special skill or hobby that can be presented occasionally in your child's new arrangement? You'd be surprised how many employers will let you rearrange your lunch hour or schedule vacation time to accommodate an occasional afternoon off so you can participate in your child's program. The more notice you give, the better your chances of getting the time off.

There are lots of ways to stay involved whether you make a personal appearance or provide support in other ways. The important thing that will be conveyed to your child is your sense of involvement.

Staying on the alert simply means that you can't let your guard down. The two best precautions a parent can use in evaluating whether or not a child care arrangement is working is to *watch* and *listen*. Look for nonverbal clues that your child may be having a difficult time, such as changes in eating or sleeping habits or unusual reluctance in going to child care, and listen to what your child is saying about her day.

> Rather than asking "How was your day?" or "What did you do today?" try asking open-ended questions such as "What was the best thing that happened to you today? What was the worst?"
>
> If you're concerned that your child isn't making friends, ask "Who did you sit next to at lunch today?"
>
> If you're still unsure about the adjustment, try asking one friend over during the weekend to see how your child does one-on-one.

All of these techniques keep you on the alert for possible problems as well as providing an opportunity for praise. Make it a point to know the names of the other children in your child's group. See if you can get a phone list so the kids can call each other—they love it! A phone list will also give you a resource of other parents to call should you have concerns to share or projects to coordinate. Who knows, maybe you'll meet someone who would love to be a backup in case your child has the sniffles on a day you simply can't miss work.

The benefits of developing an action plan to solve your child care dilemma are numerous. It's a way to prioritize tasks, organize your time, break a huge task into small manageable steps and stay on top of your responsibilities. Most of all—once it's on paper, you can forget it until it's time to deal with it!

9

EMPLOYER-SPONSORED CHILD CARE

In 1979, 110 companies in the United States offered on-site child care. Ten years later, over 4,500 companies offered an on-site child care benefit. This doesn't include companies that offer child care assistance in other forms. Clearly, child care is good business, or employers wouldn't be motivated to address the child care issue.

Child care is no longer just a women's issue. In a Portland, Oregon survey of 8,000 employees from 22 companies, it was found that 59% of female workers with children under 12 had difficulty finding child care. These women missed an average of 12 work days a year, whereas men, regardless of whether or not they had children, only missed an average of eight days per year. At first glance, you might assume that this clearly labels child care as a women's issue, but upon closer examination, it appears that the reason men have lower absenteeism is because they generally take less responsibility for child care. It's the mothers who are taking the time off to look for child care, stay home when the kids are sick or rush off to an emergency. The men miss less time because the women are taking care of the problem.

We still have a long way to go with employer awareness about the child care problem, even though more women are moving into decision-making management positions and waiting longer to begin their own families. Twenty-five years ago, the president of the company was likely to be a man with a wife who stayed home with the kids while he ran things. His perspective and ability to relate to the problems of child care would be limited compared to the "thirtysomething" female executive of today who may even be sporting executive maternity clothes herself. Yes, we've come a long way, but we've got a long road ahead of us.

For example, a Harvard University seminar for executives had the participants estimate how many of their employees were in families in which the male was the sole support of his stay-at-home wife and children. The answers ranged from 40% to an incredible 70%! Of all U.S. families, however, only about 10% fit into that traditional description.

There are many statistics available about the increase in the number of women in the workforce. In 1990, 65% of the people entering the workforce either as new workers or re-entering workers will be women. Working women of childbearing age will make up 80% of all working women. About 60% of married men have wives who work full- or part-time.

Employers can no longer ignore the societal changes that have developed and that make child care a top concern! It affects *everyone*, not just the families involved; and it's in the employer's best interest to recognize the impact of good child care and to promote successful problem-solving techniques. By ignoring the problem, the employer jeopardizes the bottom line in business: profit.

I'm not alone in predicting that child care will be *the* employee benefit of the next century, on equal footing with medical, dental and vision care. The American Society for Personnel Administration cites that "while most medium-size and large companies still lack child care policies, they, too, may join the crowd. Half of all American companies are considering offering child care benefits."

Phyllis Silverman, a consultant who advises companies on their family policies says, "The question becomes 'what are you going to do to keep that person there?' The cost of benefits becomes relative." It won't be a matter of offering help with child care to make a company stand out—it will be necessary to keep pace with the competition!

What's in It for the Employer?

As we've already mentioned, child care will become crucial if companies plan to remain competitive in the marketplace. Quality people are hard to find and sometimes hard to keep; therefore, having a child care plan can increase recruiting. One Big Eight accounting firm spends from $22,000 to $55,000 to recruit one new employee! Given a choice between two equally attractive companies, which one do you think the employee will go with if one company offers help with child care and the other doesn't?

High morale is another big bonus to employers offering help with child care. People feel better about their jobs and their relationships with their employers. My former employer had a sick leave policy which included the option of using my sick leave to care for my ill child when necessary. The loyalty I felt toward my company was invaluable in exchange for support in this area. Employers in the past had put me into a position of lying about my being ill when Lyndsay was the one with chicken pox. By recognizing the reality of family-life and work-life conflicts, both my employer and I treated each other with dignity.

As one of our examples in an earlier chapter demonstrates, productivity and quality can be affected by lack of quality child care. As an employer, would you rather have your employees thinking about their job or worrying about children coming home to an empty house? Lots of time is lost between 3:30 and 5:00 P.M. when the kids come home from school, and what little does get accomplished may not be an employee's best work because of distraction.

When an employer helps with child care, absenteeism, tardiness and turnover all decrease while recruitment and productivity increases. It just makes sense.

Perhaps the biggest contribution an employer can make in any benefits package is to reduce the overall stress of the employee. It's now quite acceptable to have a drug or alcohol recovery assistance program for employees as well as help for personal problems such as divorce and separation or even bereavement counseling. Additionally, more and more employers are adding *dependent care assistance,* which includes elderly care as well as child care, to their benefits package.

Range of Employer Options

The first step toward employer-sponsored assistance with child care is the acknowledgment that child care is a big issue with employees. If your company has the ostrich approach to dealing with child care ("if I don't acknowledge it, it doesn't exist"), this may be difficult.

In my experience in talking to different companies about child care, I've discovered that the first barrier to communication lies in the fact that employers think child care involvement means providing an on-site child care center for their employees. They are surprised to hear me say that, except in a small number of cases, this isn't usually a good solution unless you have a very stable workforce. Sometimes it can take two years from the time of the feasibility study until the grand opening of the on-site child care center, so you have to either be sure that the employees responding to the survey will still be around to use the center or confident that business is such that new workers will have similar needs.

Once employers realize that they don't necessarily have to go into the child care business to help their employees, they let their guard down and become curious. The rest is a matter of providing information.

Resource and Referral Services

One of the soundest business investments in terms of return on investment for an employer is incorporating the use of a resource and referral service to help their employees find suitable child care.

If you're lucky enough to be living in a city that offers this service, it will be listed under "Child Care" in the yellow pages. Nonprofit R&R services can assist with feasibility studies and work with employees on a one-to-one basis or in groups to help solve their child care dilemmas.

Employers also can consider the option of hiring a child care consultant for a fee if a nonprofit R&R service is unavailable or unable to meet the needs of the employer. Being nonprofit unfortunately sometimes means having a limited staff.

A child care consultant first meets with the company personnel director. Together, they devise a feasibility study which can be as simple as the following memo:

TO: All staff

FROM: Personnel

DATE: October 15, 1999

SUBJECT: Child Care

To better meet the needs of staff, ABC Company is considering providing the services of a child care consultant to assist employees with finding quality child care arrangements. Please check the appropriate box and return to Personnel by October 22 with your comments. Use extra paper if necessary.

The results of this survey will be discussed at the month-end staff meeting.

_____ yes, I would be interested

_____ no, I'm not interested

Comments:

Name, department, extension (optional):

More extensive feasibility studies can also be conducted to explore such factors as the number of commute miles of the employee, cost and satisfaction level of current child care and time lost from work due to child care-related circumstances. The more detail involved, the more important the anonymity factor to insure honest answers.

After the feasibility study is analyzed by the child care consultant, several options are presented to the employer based on these results.

On-Site Care

The cost factor may be prohibitive in some cases for this option until the employer compares it with how much it costs *not* to have an on-site center.

For example, the Union Bank in Monterey Park, California, estimates that it saved between $138,000 and $232,000 *in one year* by running an on-site child care facility! They compared the absenteeism of the bank employees who used the center with the absenteeism rates of parents who used other forms of child care during its first year of operation and found that workers using the center were absent 1.7 days less per year than other parents. These same parents had a turnover rate of 2.2% while parents who used other forms of child care had a turnover rate of 9.5%.

Any company employing large numbers of women, especially companies requiring shift work, can greatly benefit by considering on-site child care as an employee benefit. An on-site child care center can be run as an extension of the company, or the company may choose to help with start-up costs but leave the day-to-day responsibility and management of the center to a third party.

Consortium Centers

Developers are offering this option to employers in large industrial parks as "the best of all worlds." Several companies get together and underwrite a new child care center to be shared by employees of these companies. The larger the investment, the more slots that company gets for its people.

Many large national child care centers and organizations are experienced in the development and operation of consortium centers for use in housing developments as well as by corporations. Again, it just makes sense that if you build a large housing development targeted for young families, you have to consider the needs of two-income families. The beauty of neighborhood child care centers is the sense of community. Your kid's best friends in the neighborhood may also be in their group at the child care center.

Some consortium centers, like Childcare Inc., in Portland, Maine, are able to further defray costs for members by having the members contribute services rather than cash. In this case, the hospital pledged food, an architectural firm designed the space, and a law firm assisted in purchasing a suitable building.

Depending on the location of the on-site center and the needs of the company or companies involved, the center can also contribute to the community by offering open slots to the public.

Centers that have provisions for mildly-ill children more than justify the extra effort and money it takes to offer this service, especially when you consider that some employees, like attorneys, cost the company up to $200 per hour when they miss work!

There are many companies that deserve recognition for their on-site centers, including the famous Stride-Rite Corporation, in Cambridge,

Massachusetts, which began its on-site center in 1971! But without a doubt, one of the best programs I've encountered involves a sportswear firm in Ventura, California, called Patagonia. Not only does it have two wonderful on-site centers for its employees' children from ages eight weeks to 14 years, but it also provides generous parental and health benefits.

The company's president, Yvon Chouinard, is quick to admit the child care center is profit motivated: He feels it keeps five to 10 people a year from quitting, thus saving the company lots of money.

Family Day Care Home Networks

What if the majority of the employees don't need child care or the feasibility study indicates that parents would be more apt to use an off-site family day care home?

The child care consultant can work with individual parents to find suitable family day care homes near work or home or even coordinate (with the appropriate licensing agency) a training program to recruit and encourage more family day care homes in an area of need.

Employers can help by buying slots in family day care homes for their employees' children or even holding slots open for emergency child care, such as when a child is mildly ill.

The child care consultant prescreens family day care homes in the area to better assist the parent in decision-making, rather than just handing out telephone numbers. It's easier and more responsible to promote a family day care home that you have personally visited and approved.

Cafeteria-Style Benefits

My former employer has what is called a cafeteria style child care benefit.

Cafeteria-style benefits means that you choose which benefits to take advantage of. Maybe you have health coverage under your husband's policy and would rather use health benefits offered by your employer towards something else. If not child care, then maybe employer-paid membership in a health club or some other alternative benefit.

My child care expenses were $200 per month. My employer deducted $200 from my paycheck at the beginning of the month, then gave it back to me at the end of the month as an employee benefit to assist with child care. Because it was an employee benefit, it was considered nontaxable income. This translated into a tax savings at the end of the year on $2,400! Spread this out over time, and you can see how it would quickly add up.

This is a creative solution for employers who have a mix of personnel and want to offer an equitable plan for parents as well as nonparents.

Help with Logistics

Employers can solve transportation problems by providing a van to pick up employees' kids from school and drop them off at on-site or near-site child care.

Employers can help with school vacation periods by contributing to organizations such as the YMCA in exchange for slots.

Flextime

By allowing employees control over their start and stop times, employers can alleviate a tremendous amount of stress. The secret is in great communication.

Employers establish core times when everyone must be at work to keep the business running smoothly. However, by varying the start and stop times (8:00–5:00 or 7:30–4:30 or 9:00–6:00), parents are able to better coordinate child care arrangements.

Another form of flextime is the 10/40 plan where the workday is 10 hours long for four days—Monday through Thursday or Tuesday through Friday—equaling a 40-hour work week, with overtime being paid for hours in excess of 40 hours per week, rather than in excess of eight hours per day.

Flextime also allows for parent conferences during the day as well as the opportunity to do volunteer work in the child's school or child care center. The parent either makes up the time or uses vacation hours.

This system, like all others, has the potential for abuse, which is why communication is so vital.

Workers without children have access to the same options to be used at their discretion. Maybe you've always wanted to take a particular class, but it's only offered during the day. Flextime would give you the opportunity to do it.

One employee I know of left work early once a week (with the employer's full knowledge and blessing) to take ballet lessons. The employer knew the value of encouraging balance in the life of a stressed-out key employee. This same employee was the recipient of an employer-paid housekeeper during the final stages of a huge project that took everything she had to complete on time. By eliminating some of the stress at home, she was able to complete the project on time and within budget.

Job Sharing

The concept of job sharing is fairly simple: two people sharing one job, each also sharing benefits. This works extremely well for people who want to spend more time with their children but don't want to give up their work completely or lose their place in the company.

If you're interested in job sharing, first find someone with the same skills and abilities who is also very familiar with your job duties. Another employee who is contemplating leaving the company to spend more time at home is a natural choice.

Next, draw up a proposal listing all the reasons it would work. *If you can demonstrate how the company will benefit from the arrangement, you're halfway there.* Make an appointment with your supervisor to present the proposal and ask for feedback. You have to get it through the chain of command in proper order, so don't skip to the president of the company until you've thoroughly discussed the proposal with all the people in between. If you can sell your supervisor on the idea, she can do a better job of selling it to the personnel manager.

Don't forget to include a trial period in your proposal, giving your employer the option of changing his mind if things don't work out, but make the trial period long enough to give the arrangement a chance.

The proposal idea works well for exploring flextime as well as job sharing.

Part-Time Jobs

More employers are offering part-time work with prorated benefits as a means of attracting and keeping good people. A part-time job works well for parents because it allows them to balance their career and family obligations. The company benefits in employee loyalty and productivity. Should things change at home, the employee has the option of switching to full-time work without losing seniority or benefits.

Other companies allow the employee to structure work time between home and the office. Lots of work can be done on a home computer just as easily as in the workplace. If the employee knows this is an option when his child wakes up with a fever, he can more easily accommodate his family needs and still accomplish some work on projects while at home.

Conclusion

As you can see, there are a wide variety of options available to employers who want to provide help with child care. I firmly believe the number one drawback is lack of awareness about what's available. If more employers knew how child care impacts business, we would see more employer involvement.

There is a solution to every child care problem, and the employer *can* be involved.

Whether the employer begins by taking small steps or jumps right in with an on-site center, becoming involved in child care is just plain good business.

BIBLIOGRAPHY

Andrews, Lori B. "Employers Who Help Companies That Care." *Parents*, October 1983, 32.

Associated Press. "Consulting Firm Aiming at Corporate Child Care Options," *Highlander* (newspaper), April 5, 1989.

———, "Keeping Employees Happy: Sportswear Firm Beefs Up Benefits to Boost Worker Contentment." *Los Angeles Daily News*, April 23, 1989.

Friedman, Dana E. "Special Report: Child Care for Employees' Kids." *The Harvard Business Review*, March–April, 1986.

The Los Angeles Business Journal. "Study Said Bank Saved Money By Operating Day Care Center." April 3, 1989.

Lundberg, Kirsten O. "More Firms Involved in Day Care." *The Sacramento Bee*, April 2, 1989.

Morrison, George S. *Early Childhood Education Today.* 4th ed. Columbus, Ohio: Merrill, 1988.

Ostroff, Ron. "Corporate Child Care: Growing Up." *Los Angeles Daily News*, March 20, 1989.

Sherlock, John. "A Look at Statistics That Shape the Nation: Hospitals Lead in Child Care." *USA Today*, March 17, 1989.

Jarvis, Elena. "Employer Commitment to Child Care Is Crucial." *Ventura Star Free Press*, March 7, 1989.

10
DEALING WITH GUILT

It's 5:30 in the morning, according to the lighted dial on the clock. The rest of the world is still deep in slumber as Joanie rouses herself out of a warm bed to pad heavily into the bathroom and stare at the mirror. Judging from the dark circles under her eyes, it's not hard to believe that she got up three times last night with the baby.

"I look fifty," she mutters to herself.

A familiar voice inside her head says, "Fifty-five, on a good day."

Normally, Joanie takes a shower at night so the next morning she can throw a load of wash in the washing machine before her husband is up and ready to take his shower—the water heater can only take on one project at a time. Today she has to decide between laundry and washing her hair because she was simply too tired last night to do either one.

One cup of coffee later, the world is beginning to look familiar again: dirty dishes in the sink to be cleared, rinsed and loaded into the dishwasher; school lunches to be made and packed (she tried making them the night before, but the kids complained about stale bread); homework to be checked and stuffed into book bags; clean clothes to be found for herself and the kids; the cat, fish and hamster to be fed; the newspaper to be read—but only the front page (no time for more!); breakfast to be laid out. And then it is time for what she really dreads—wake-up detail.

For some reason, from the time Joanie was a little girl, she could not stand the idea of waking people up out of a sound sleep. Even though the adult Joanie believed it was her responsibility to make sure everyone was where they had to be and on time, it still distressed her to have to be the one to rouse them out of their dreams every weekday.

She had an especially hard time with waking her husband. In the first place, he was a sound, sound sleeper—he almost never heard the children if they called out during the night. Although gentle in nature, Joanie had resorted to threats to get him out of bed in the morning (her favorite fantasy was pouring a pitcher full of frozen pennies on him if he didn't heed the first two warnings).

Secondly, Joanie could not understand why a 44-year-old man needed help getting up in the morning, and she deeply resented his insistent helplessness.

After prodding, coaxing, and demanding Steve to get his bones off the mattress, Joanie once gave up and let him suffer the consequences of sleeping late. As a result, Steve missed an important meeting—which Joanie had no way of knowing about ahead of time—and punished her by bringing it up during every argument for the next six months.

"I still can't believe you made me miss that meeting."

He finally wore her down with his whining, and she apologized and promised to never let it happen again.

So every morning at 7:00, Joanie brings Steve a cup of coffee, which is usually cold by the time he finally pries his fingers off the sheets. She's learned to open the curtains, turn on the radio, start the water running for his shower and sit on the bed with her hand on his shoulder, calling his name until he responds to her warning about running out of hot water.

And every morning, Joanie, who honestly loves her husband at just about every other time of the day or night, plots different ways to eliminate him off the face of the earth because he doesn't exercise more self-discipline.

With Steve out of bed and grumpily making his way to the bathroom, Joanie concentrates on the kids. Ten-year-old Tommy isn't too tough—he's a natural early bird, and nine times out of 10 is already dressed by the time Joanie opens his door.

But Kylie, her middle child, is another story. Joanie sensed during her pregnancy that Kylie would be a night owl, so she shouldn't have been surprised when Kylie (nicknamed Oscar after the *Sesame Street* grouch) became almost as difficult as Steve to wake up in the mornings. No matter how much preparation time they put in the night before, mornings were a nightmare. Joanie secretly harbored resentment over Kylie's foul moods even though she also felt somehow responsible.

Baby Corey was the easiest to deal with. Always cheerful, sweet-faced and seemingly eager to please Mom, Corey was a bright spot in an otherwise horrible routine.

As Steve and the kids finish breakfast, Joanie escapes into the bathroom to try to pull herself together for work. It is one of the few times she's able to focus on her own needs, rather than on someone else's. She is over the hump: They are all up and reasonably ready. She has done it again.

After dropping off the two older kids at school and the baby at his family day care home, Joanie makes her way to work through rush hour traffic, three and one-half hours after waking.

"There has *got* to be a better way to live," she thinks.

"If you were a good mother, you'd stay home with the kids and make do on one salary. It was good enough for your mother, it should be good enough for you. Is work more important than seeing your children grow up? Besides, other mothers work and still manage to volunteer in their children's classes, bake cookies and greet their husbands at the front door wrapped only in cellophane."

The voice inside her head had been around for so long that it no longer surprises Joanie to hear it's on-going laundry list of faults.

"Yeah, but I'm not my mother. I've got a great job that I love which also keeps me sane enough to handle things at home—and besides, we need my income to make ends meet."

"But think how much you'd save if you stayed home with the kids. No more child care costs, lunches in expensive restaurants or hurried trips to the store every night. And think of the money you'd save on clothes alone! Admit it! You'd rather dress up every day and conduct meetings than stay home with your babies! Shame on you! When are you going to grow up and stop being so selfish. Everyone knows a good mother puts her family above all else. If you quit, you'd be there when they came home from school with cookies and milk, maybe even become a Brownie leader. Kylie would stop hitting other kids, and Corey would know what it would be like to have a real mother."

"And then there's Steve. You could be there for him instead of feeling like a drill sergeant."

Lately, the voice has been making sense, which frightens Joanie because another voice deep down inside her, the one that says, "You're doing okay, honey. In fact, you're doing great," is only a whisper.

Joanie had absolutely no idea which voice was right, so she tried ignoring them both until it felt like her head would split in half.

It didn't take long to realize she couldn't continue this way. With the help of a counselor (available through her employer's employee assistance program), Joanie began to unravel her personal guilt web and quiet the negative voices that undermined her confidence.

What Is Guilt?

We have all experienced feeling guilty. It's a normal, healthy way to keep ourselves in check. Guilt sometimes applies the brakes when we're heading in a certain direction by creating a discomfort that forces us to look at our actions. Sometimes, though, it only causes us to take our feet off the accelerator.

A feeling of guilt can be caused by different factors in different people. For example, if you were driving in the middle of nowhere at 3:00 in the morning and came across a red light, would you stop? After stopping, would you wait for a green light even if you knew there were no cars coming? Would you feel guilty for running the red light or only if you were caught?

It's interesting to note that the dictionary's first definition of guilt has to do with the commission of a crime rather than an internal reaction when our actions are incongruous with our value system. But it also lists self-reproach caused by imagined misconduct. In other words, it doesn't matter how much you can justify working, if your guts say you should be staying home with your kids, you will experience guilt.

Getting a Grip on Guilt

The first step in dealing with guilt is to isolate the event that triggered the guilt.

What is it that's causing you to feel guilty, and how often does it happen? How long does the guilt last? Do you feel just awful after dropping the kids off at school in the morning but snap out of it once you reach your office? Or are you plagued with guilt throughout the day, making concentration difficult and pleasure virtually impossible?

It helps to keep a journal for three weeks to see not only when you feel guilty but also when you feel pretty good about things. Note such things as diet, amount of sleep, stressors and anything else that flows out of the pen. Be patient at first if this task seems difficult, especially if it's been a while since you've used your writing skills. Most people come to look forward to making journal entries once they develop the habit.

If you live with other people, be absolutely certain that your journal is in a safe place. Nothing can inhibit writing faster than the thought of someone else reading your innermost thoughts.

Positive Guilt

Not all guilt is negative. When I decide to go to a matinee instead of working on this book, I feel guilty because I know the deadline is approaching, and I really should be at home working on chapter 10. Even though I know I deserve an afternoon off and even though the movie may give me renewed energy to finish the project, I feel guilty! Not quite guilty enough to skip the matinee but guilty enough to let it bother me while in line for the ticket. Once inside, I'm committed. I know either I can accept my decision to take a three-hour break, or I can sit there and feel absolutely miserable—and still not accomplish anything on chapter 10.

I've made a decision: A break during a stressful time is needed to accomplish my goal, so I'll take advantage of the time away to unwind. Negative guilt nags me in the ticket line ("you *should* be home writing") and won't allow me to play hooky *ever*. Positive guilt keeps me on task with the book, so I don't slack off every day.

In this case, guilt kicked in because I had two competing needs: finishing chapter 10 and escaping to the movies for a break.

Joanie felt guilty about not being Superwoman and guilty about her anger towards Steve's insensitivity and lack of involvement. She felt guilty every time Kylie hit another child, never considering that lots of kids with moms who stay home hit other kids. She felt guilty because Tommy and Corey were so sweet and easygoing that she believed she *should* be spending more quality time with them. She felt guilty about enjoying her job and looking forward to going to work every day. She felt guilty because she knew Steve wanted her to be sexier, but she was just too tired at the end of the day. Then she felt guilty about being exhausted. She felt guilty about not reading the paper every day, not cooking a hot breakfast for her family, not having all the laundry folded and put away and very guilty about being the one to have to wake everyone up every morning.

No wonder Joanie's headaches became severe enough to seek professional help!

Whose Problem Is it?

After analyzing the guilt triggers, the next step is to determine responsibility for the problem. Are you taking on someone else's job? Ask yourself, "Whose problem is this?"

Through the use of a journal or by talking it out with a good friend, determine exactly what you feel guilty about. Don't censure yourself!

For example, "I feel terribly guilty because Lyndsay is having a problem with a bully in her class. If I were a better mother, she'd know how to handle herself against him. If I were a better mother, I would have insisted that the teacher intervene. If I were a better mother, my child wouldn't suffer. My poor child has to learn about life through her own experiences because I'm a rookie and because I don't have the wisdom to know how to guide her away from pain."

You can see how writing out the problem and letting yourself get carried away with guilt can actually clarify the issues. The source of the guilt is the fact that I can't be by my daughter's side throughout life, insulating her from reality. Determining ownership is easy: It's Lyndsay's problem. I can help her through it, but it's something for which she has to find the answers by herself.

In Joanie's case, whose problem is it that Steve can't roll out of bed without a Broadway production every morning? It's Steve's. If Joanie died tomorrow, Steve would learn to get out of bed on time. Steve played on her guilt to escape responsibility, and she bought it!

And if the kids don't like stale sandwiches, they have the option of making their own lunches or buying from the cafeteria. Obviously, Joanie wasn't the only one who thought she was a doormat. Once her husband and the kids realized she was not going to allow herself to be treated like a doormat, it was relatively easy to retrain their acquired helplessness.

The funny thing is, you would never guess that Joanie is the same person who coordinates a large personnel department for a major firm in San Francisco. This "doormat" supervises a variety of projects with efficiency, warmth and professionalism. None of Joanie's co-workers would recognize her at home. So what's the difference between work and home?

At work, Joanie evaluates tasks based on what needs to be done and who has the skill or the time to complete them. In other words, she delegates without the slightest tinge of guilt. If someone doesn't do their job, she holds them responsible, not herself.

Another example of identifying problem ownership is Joanie's feelings about being a working mother. The voice she keeps hearing sounds very much like her mother's voice, if she listens carefully. It's Joanie's problem to come to terms with her parenting style which is quite different from her mother's stay-at-home style.

By writing out all of the pros and cons of working versus staying home with her children, Joanie came to the conclusion that it's possible for her to work and still be a good mother. She doesn't have to bake bread or iron sheets (my mom even ironed underwear!) to earn the love of her children. One she accepted that her lifestyle was different, but every bit as valid as the concept with which she had grown up, Joanie was better able to deal with the daily tasks that usually induced so much guilt.

Finally, she took a long hard look at her three beautiful children and was shocked to realize how normal they were. A bit spoiled, perhaps, but maybe that was normal now, too.

After applying some business principles at home, such as delegating responsibility, Joanie still got up at 5:30 on some mornings. But now it was to read the whole paper, write in her journal and occasionally even use some hot water for a bubble bath before work. Things got predictably worse before they got better—especially for Steve, but once he accepted the new Joanie, now a full partner instead of a doormat, their relationship improved considerably.

Joanie still had guilt, but it was healthy and manageable guilt. More for herself than for son Corey, Joanie made up for her lack of time with him by taking him on long walks through the neighborhood on Saturday morning when everyone else slept in. She realized that she and her daughter Kylie, needed more time together and initiated a "girl's night out" once a week when the two of them would go to a movie or bowling. Although her oldest son appeared to need her less (translation: he was so symptom-free that Joanie was suspicious), they went to the library together every two weeks. Joanie put her foot down with Steve, too. No more marathon tennis matches on Saturday with the guys. Reasonable limits were set with family time being a priority.

Slowly but surely, they were starting to feel like a real family. They even had Tommy's scout group over for a barbeque/games night two months ago.

The more action Joanie took, the more control she felt in her life. The more control, the less guilt; it all works together.

Once Steve began assuming responsibilities for the family, a side benefit included Joanie seeing him in a new, better light, which worked wonders for their love life. At least twice a month they hire a sitter to stay with the kids while they go on a date—guilt-free!

When You Don't Know What's Wrong

Lots of people experience "free-floating" anxiety and guilt on a daily basis. Maybe you're living day to day with little thought to the future. We all get into a rut now and then. After an appropriate wallowing, I prefer to think of a rut as the first step in making changes for the better rather than a way of life I'm powerless to change.

During my divorce, I spent my days worrying about survival. Living day to day was a way to get through the worst of it. Sometimes I lived hour-to-hour. This is different from the boredom that comes from being stuck in a rut at work or at home.

If you don't know what's wrong or where to begin, try some of these stress busters:

1. Write a long letter to yourself, catching up with all that's happened in the last few years. Include the high as well as the low points. Just the process of listing events can sometimes produce perspective. Don't forget to include such things as future plans and dreams. Brag about your husband and kids, too!
2. Even though it may be the last thing you feel like doing, take a long, brisk walk through the neighborhood. If it's cold and windy, so much the better. You can reward yourself with a hot cup of something when you get home. Trade off watching the neighbor's kids so yours can be in good hands while you escape on a regular basis. Walking is a great way to clear the cobwebs out.
3. Take care of all the things within your control first. No one thinks twice if a man hires a housekeeper to come in and bail him out, right? If you're coming home to a depressing display of unfinished chores, it's worth the money to hire help. Think about it.

4. Keep in touch with people who make you feel good. If you don't know anyone like that, figure out a way to expand or begin your circle of friends. It's not at all unusual to realize most of your friends are centered around your husband's friends or are spouses of his friends. It's okay to have a friend of your own.
5. What have you always wanted to do? Do it.
6. Instead of making a "to do" list, make a "done" list at the end of the day. You'll be amazed at the amount of work you accomplished. There's always tomorrow for the leftovers.
7. Sit down with your husband or best friend and plan a dream vacation, one that is with or without children along. Decide how much you need to save each month to make that trip a reality. Even if it takes two years to get to Hawaii, just knowing you have a plan will help you through some of the rough times. In the meantime, start collecting brochures and looking forward to your vacation—you deserve it! Working with a travel agent can help, as many now have videos for loan of different destinations.
8. Play hooky once in a while. If you can, get a cohort to do the same, and the two of you can go to a matinee after lunch together! One friend took a vacation day every Wednesday during the winter to catch a ski bus to a ski resort. Believe me, she was so appreciative that she actually worked much harder and accomplished more in her four-day week than most people did in five. An alternate plan would be to spring your child from school on a slow day and finally take in the zoo or museum! The other obvious option would be to involve your husband (wife) or boyfriend (girlfriend) in forbidden fun. Somehow, just knowing everyone else is at work or school makes your escape just that much sweeter. Where would you go and what would you do, if you could?
9. Find a support group by calling the city, county or state mental health department and explaining your situation. If a support group isn't available, consider setting up your own on a formal or informal basis. Or better yet, call the Chamber of Commerce and ask for a community resource guide which should list such groups. Or call a "hot line" established for people in distress, and ask them where to find help. Don't eliminate the idea of seeking help one-on-one from a professional counselor. Sometimes all it takes is a few sessions to get things back in perspective. It may be just what you've been looking for. If money is a problem, there are many agencies that charge on a sliding scale or provide services for free.

One final thought on goal setting and attaining your dreams: Recently I was asked to speak to a group of local college students who were exploring the field of early childhood education. While reviewing different goal-setting techniques, one woman raised her hand and asked how on earth she could achieve her goal of operating her own family day care home—no one would rent to her under those circumstances, and she couldn't afford to buy her own home. She also didn't like the idea of working for "peanuts" in someone else's family day care home and was extremely discouraged about her future.

By focusing on goal-setting techniques, we were able to come up with a list of ways she could take control over her future and attain her dream. First, we concentrated on how she could become a home owner. She needed to educate herself on the variety of mortgage programs available. There were numerous resources for obtaining this information, including state and federal agencies as well as realtors and title companies. The important thing was to develop a workable plan to buy a home, even if it took 10 years to do so.

The next step involved analyzing her attitude about working for someone else. When I asked her if she would accept a salary for a training period before she opened her own family day care home, she replied yes with a slow smile. Ensuing discussions pointed out that it was a lot cheaper and smarter to learn while on someone else's payroll. By adjusting her attitude about working for someone else while she was moving towards her goal of opening her own family day care home, this woman began to see employment as a step toward rather than away from self-employment.

If You Still Feel Guilty . . .

I think if you believe you're doing your best in balancing work and family needs, then you probably are. If you find yourself wondering, with sadness, what kind of memories your children will have, stop and reflect on the difference in memories between you and your own parents. Chances are their childhood memories are quite different from yours.

When I was little, my mom was always there with hot tea and fresh towels, warm right out of the dryer, whenever it rained. I knew as I was walking home through the rain that she would be there, just as my daughter knows I'll always be there for her—maybe not with hot tea and warm towels after a rain but with love and concern during any problem. Lyndsay may not express her gratitude yet, but I feel it.

My parents were "different" because they spoke with thick German accents and had "old world" ideas about how children should be raised, so when they broke tradition and allowed a slumber party or showed up for a school function, I thought I would burst with pride. My daughter takes such things in stride, much to my disappointment, I must admit.

Things have changed dramatically since we were children, yet we continue to measure ourselves with our parents' yardsticks.

The point is, the memories will be different for your child, but if she feels safe, loved and valued, then you've done your job well.

Put yourself in your child's place and try to see all the positive things about your family. Work on things that need attention, then relax and enjoy being a parent.

11

LONG-TERM EFFECTS OF CHILD CARE

My personal beliefs about the long-term effects of child care on an individual can be summed up rather simply: It depends. Sorry, there are no easy answers.

In a nutshell, the long-term effects are determined by the quality of care, number of providers, experiences within the child care environment, age of child, temperaments of the child and the provider and many, many other factors, including your attitude about your child being in child care. After all, we can only *speculate* on how little Freddy would have turned out if his mom had stayed home.

I believe good child care, like good parenting, produces positive effects. As you struggle with your own questions, you have to reach way down inside yourself and analyze your situation. My daughter's pediatrician once said that parents make thousands of decisions on a regular basis about the welfare of their children, and if they're very lucky, most of them will be good decisions—and kids will survive 99.9% of the regrettable ones.

Your children's perceptions of childhood trauma may surprise you. If you don't believe me, just ask your parents what they think scarred you the most. They may remember old wounds having to do with canceled trips to Disneyland while you remember the day your mom made you wear those awful shoes to school. The point is, right now you have no way of knowing which areas your adult children will say you needed to work on. It will be interesting 20 years from now when you ask them about it over coffee. But it's hard to predict, so do your best and have faith.

I'd be willing to bet that you're probably doing a much better job of parenting than you think you are.

Early Studies

The negative effects of early separation have been studied extensively as they relate to residential institutions rather than quality child care centers. One 1946 study by René Spitz actually involved infants in foundling homes (homes for abandoned and illegitimate babies) raised by caregivers (with a 1:8 ratio of caregivers to infants). These babies were compared with infants raised by their mothers in prison! The prison mothers were all either emotionally disturbed or mentally retarded. Even under these severe conditions, the babies raised by prison mothers fared far better than the foundling home babies. According to the study, deviant maternal care was better than institutional care.

Another study reported in 1952 by John Bowlby concluded that any break in the mother/child relationship could have severe consequences. By "any break," Bowlby was referring to loss of mother due to death or separation from mother due to hospitalization, employment or neglect. These kids were more apt to be depressed, retarded (physically or mentally) or delinquent.

You can imagine how this type of data can be construed to apply to day care in general rather than to the specific situations of the studies. Regardless, the early messages were clear: Unless mom stayed home and cared for the children, they were doomed—misfits—degenerates.

This was also the time when the sins of the child were visited upon the mother. If Johnny was a sissy, it was because his mother coddled him too much. If Johnny was a bully, it was because his mother couldn't control him. Now the same arguments are being used for mothers who stay home versus mothers who work outside the home. We can't win! The parents (usually the mothers) are held accountable for the successes or failures of their children. Sound familiar?

A 30-year study finished in 1966 by Harold Skeels concluded that it is the care and nurturance that affect children's development, not the person who provides it. Skeels came upon this information by comparing 25 infants who were institutionalized because they were thought to be mentally retarded. Half of the group were transferred to another institution where they were cared for by a group of retarded women who lavished attention on them. The other half of the group remained institutionalized where they were.

Thirty years later, Skeels did a follow-up study and found that of the group that received early nurturance, 11 out of 13 infants had been adopted by families, and 12 out of 13 had gone on to receive an education and become self-supporting adults whose children had average IQs! The fate of the infants who remained in the original institution and had their custodial needs but none of their nurturance needs met was dramatically different. Of the original 12 infants left in this institution,

11 survived. Four of these were still in institutions as adults, another was a vagrant, and the remaining six included a gardener's assistant at the very institution that raised him, three dishwashers, one part-time worker in a cafeteria and one domestic worker.

The conclusion was that care and nurturance can be provided by someone other than the mother, and the child will develop normally. This leads me to believe that if kids raised by people with mental handicaps did okay, then surely my child has a good shot at life when exposed to a quality child care program. That program is staffed by educated, loving individuals and includes developmentally appropriate activities and toys, parent involvement and lots of socialization opportunities with other kids.

Current Studies

In a fascinating article by Ellen Galinsky and Deborah Phillips entitled "The Day Care Debate," several factors contributing to long-term effects of child care were discussed.

The authors tried to answer the question: Does being in child care affect a child's attachment to his mother? Their research seemed to come to the same conclusions as the majority of works I've read on the subject: It depends.

They cite two famous studies which conclude infants who began child care for more than 20 hours a week in their first year were more likely to be classified as insecurely attached to their mothers than children who spent less time in infant care or who started later.

That's just what parents *didn't* want to hear.

A test called the Strange Situation was developed by Mary Ainsworth, Ph.D. and her colleagues at Johns Hopkins University to assess attachment. They put infants between the ages of 12 and 18 months into different situations and recorded their reactions when their mothers returned after having previously left the room. Three-minute episodes were observed in this order:

1. Mom carries the infant to the playroom and puts him or her down.
2. A stranger arrives and tries to play with the baby.
3. Mom leaves the room.
4. Mom returns, and the stranger leaves.
5. Mom leaves, and the infant is alone.
6. The stranger returns.
7. Mom returns.

"Secure attachment" infants experienced a reduction in stress and were able to return to play and exploration after mom came back.

"Insecure/avoidant attachment" infants avoided contact with the mother or continued to play when the mother returned.

"Secure/resistant attachment" infants didn't want anything to do with mom or failed to be comforted by her presence when she returned—yet still tried to remain close to her.

Kids in child care more than 20 hours a week tended to be insecurely attached to their mothers, according to this study.

It's important to note that these studies can often be viewed in different ways. For example, the controversy in this study revolves around several elements:

- There are other factors at work besides whether or not the infant has experienced child care. Babies, like all humans, are multifaceted.
- Interpretation of data may vary. Infants who are secure may not find this situation to be stressful, so the need for comfort becomes unnecessary. This could be misinterpreted as avoidance.
- Other research may be contradictory. Alison Clarke-Stewart, Ph.D., a psychologist from the University of California, Irvine, who has been studying the effects of child care on children, suggests that the "insecure" infants in the Strange Situation actually signaled greater maturity, not insecurity.

Effects on Mom

The first time my child ran to her preschool teacher and in the process ran *away* from me, I had mixed emotions. I applauded Lyndsay's security and ability to make attachments outside the family, yet I wondered, with a slight pang, if I was being replaced. I'm sure every parent has faced this dilemma at one point or another, and I'm sure I'll face it to lesser degrees the rest of my life. Isn't that why people cry at high school graduations and weddings?

The good news is that no one can take mom's place.

Stop and ask yourself who the child runs to when she falls down. Who does she call to in the middle of the night?

As we've seen earlier, some studies show that kids in a quality day care program can attach to their mothers much in the same way as kids whose mothers are at home with them. Yes, kids do form attachments to their caregivers (if they don't, then there's a problem), but they still prefer Mom.

Kids feel attached to people who make them feel safe; this includes the provider, father, siblings and grandparents. Some attachments are stronger than others, but they all make the child feel secure, which is an important goal in infancy.

It's easy to feel threatened if you think your child appears more attached to her provider than to you—especially if the child is great at preschool and turns into a monster the minute you head out the door for the ride home. Don't forget that many children have a letdown at the end of the day. After all, they've been following rules and stifling impulses for hours. If you can see this letdown as a positive sign, it will be easier to deal with.

What about the child who gives Mom the cold shoulder at the end of the day? Nothing cuts through the heart of an already guilty mom as much as having a child look right through her when she's been looking forward to a hug all afternoon. Hard as it may be, that is the time to be patient, loving and available to the child until he's ready to let you back in. You can acknowledge his feelings by commenting, "You look angry." You can allow the child to vent his emotions by listening in a nonjudgmental way. Now is not the time to launch into a tirade about your daily pressures. Just give him a chance to be heard and acknowledged. If he doesn't want to talk about how he feels, say something like, "When you want to talk, I'll be in the kitchen. I could sure use a helper."

Pay close attention if you feel threatened by your child's provider. Remember, the provider is a member of your team rather than someone jockeying for power.

As we've seen time and time again, there's only one mom.

Are expectations different for men and women concerning child care? You bet they are. That might explain why women may be more affected by child care.

The *Washington Post* ran an article by Carol Krucoff that caught my eye entitled, "Day Care: Baby May Do OK but Will Mom Survive?"

Ms. Krucoff quotes an expert in child development issues, T. Berry Brazelton, a pediatrician, professor and author. Dr. Brazelton is worried about the sense of loss and inadequacy some moms feel who have children in child care. To protect themselves, they may turn off the emotional development that commonly occurs when a woman becomes a new mother.

Another researcher, Sandra Scarr, author of *Mother Care—Other Care,* which won a National Psychology Award for Excellence in the Media in 1985, spent seven years studying the effects of day care and 20 years researching child development and the factors that determine intelligence and personality. She concluded that a child can have a relationship with more than one person! She believes too much emphasis is placed on the exclusive relationship between mother and child. In fact, she goes on to say that "mothering isn't all baking brownies and cheery outings. There are a lot of incompetent, upset and depressed mothers taking out their boredom and frustration on their kids."

It's a sobering thought but certainly worth consideration.

Aggression

Studies show that, generally speaking, kids who have been in a child care program are more socially competent, more self-confident, more outgoing and less fearful than those who have not. The same studies show that it's also true they're less polite, less respectful of others' rights, less compliant with adult demands and more aggressive and hostile to others.

I think it's safe to say that child care, in and of itself, is not the singular cause of children's anxiety or aggression. Rather, it is a child's temperament, ability to attach and numerous other factors that will determine aggressiveness.

Will your child gain the benefits of a quality child care program or turn into an aggressive, selfish brat? There are obviously more factors to consider in determining the cause of aggression than whether or not the child has had child care.

Are Kids in Child Care Smarter?

All things being equal (which they never are), kids who attend day care programs perform higher on some tests than kids who do not. A part-time program for children aged two and one-half to five can help your child be more verbally expressive and interactive with adults.

Kindergarten today asks more of its children than when you and I were five. Children in preschool programs are better able to meet the challenges of kindergarten.

Another study, however, showed that scores on tests of perception, language and intelligence were lower for two-year-old children attending day care than for children being cared for at home. The children in this study, though, had been in a day care situation since they were less than eight-weeks-old where the adult/child ratios were an astronomical 1:16 and 1:24!

The Effects of Child Care on the Family

The need for quality child care is a reality for many families. There is simply no choice. Once society accepts this premise and stops passing judgment, families can get on with doing what needs to be done to survive.

Let's assume that the parent has explored all the options and come to the conclusion that a child care program is what's needed at this time and within certain parameters. How could this affect the rest of the family? The positive effects might include:

❖ Working outside the home is made possible for Mom. Financial stress is reduced. The entire family may breathe a sigh of relief.

- ❖ Or perhaps child care permits Mom to finish her education, which will open up future employment opportunities as well as being extremely satisfying.
- ❖ Child care can provide a welcome break in parenting duties for a parent, stressed by either work or personal problems. The child is actually better off in a safe, child-oriented place for part of the day—Parents aren't the only ones who benefit from child care.
- ❖ Leisure activities without children can be planned and enjoyed without guilt if the parents are confident that their child is thriving in their absence.

People are quick to discuss the negative aspects of child care, but you can see it's possible for a family to benefit greatly from a quality child care program.

Reduction of stress, regardless of its source, can produce positive results for any family.

Final Thoughts

To those of you who have the luxury of choice, I have full faith and confidence in your ability to make a child care choice that is consistent with your values. It's the parents who feel they have no choice that I especially want to encourage. Therefore, I admit to a certain bias when it comes to child care. I think good child care combined with good parenting helps make good children.

I hate hearing horror stories about child care producing unfeeling little robots who are unable to have lasting adult relationships and who have one foot in the grave from exposure to a host of diseases and the other on a banana peel.

We simply can't make blanket statements about child care being good or bad for every child in every situation—*too many people need quality, affordable, accessible child care*. This includes not just people who need to be employed outside the home to meet their bills every month but also people who want to provide another method of socialization for their children and people who need a break to maintain their sanity.

I believe all child care is temporary and part-time. Even kids who are in child care all day still go home to their parents and spend weekends, holidays and other concentrations of time with their families. The family unit is still the most important aspect of a child's life. Many factors that have very little to do with child care decide the quality of your child's life.

The truth of the matter is that no one really knows the long-term effects of child care because quality programs haven't been around long enough to produce longitudinal studies—with the exception of the Head Start program, and there the news is very good.

It makes sense that the whole child has to be considered along with all the pros and cons and a healthy dose of gut instincts.

I sincerely believe that people do what works best for them and that values change over time. You may not always feel the same way about things; it's okay to change your mind.

Based on my gut feelings as a mother and the controversial data that exists on the long-term effects of child care, I believe that everything works together: the home environment, stability of the relationships within the family, quality of child care and all the other aspects that affect quality of life.

At the risk of oversimplifying, the presence or absence of child care will have a greater impact on some children than others. Some will remember fondly, some will wish it had been different, and most will probably take it in stride.

You have to do what's best for your family, and only you know what that is.

BIBLIOGRAPHY

Berns, Roberta M. *Child, Family, Community.* 2d ed. New York: Holt, Rinehart & Winston, 1989.

Bowlby, J. *Maternal Care and Mental Health.* 2nd ed. New York: Schocken, 1966. (Originally published by World Health Organization of the United Nations, Geneva, 1952); and Bowlby, J. Attachment (Vol. 1) and Loss (Vol. 2). New York: Basic Books, 1969 and 1973.

Clarke-Stewart, K. A. & Fein, G. G. Early Childhood Programs. In P.H. Mussen (Ed.) *Handbook of Child Psychology* (Vol. 2, 4th ed.). New York: Wiley, 1983.

Galinsky, Ellen and Deborah Phillips. "The Day Care Debate." *Parents,* November 1988.

Krucoff, Carol. "Day Care: Baby May Do OK, but Will Mom Survive?" *The Washington Post*

Lazar, I. et al. The Persistence of Preschool Effects: A long follow-up of fourteen infant and preschool experiments: Summary. Washington, D.C.: U.S. Dept. of Health and Human Services, Administration for Children, Youth and Families, 1977.

Peaslee, M. V. The Development of Competency in Two Year Old Infants in Day Care and Home-reared Environments. Doctoral dissertation. Florida State University, 1976. Cited in *A. Clarke-Stewart,* 1982.

Skeels, H. M. Adult Status of Children With Contrasting Early Life Experiences. *Monographs of the Society for Research in Child Development,* 1966. 31 (3, whole no. 105)

Spitz, R. A. "Hospitalism: An Inquiry into the Genesis of Psychiatric Conditioning in Early Childhood." In D. Fenschel et al. (Eds.) *Psychoanalytic Studies of the Child* (Vol. 1). New York: International Universities Press, 1946.

A Final Note

Please write to me in care of my publisher.

I'd like to answer your questions and hear your response to this book.

If I've accomplished nothing else, I hope I have given you confidence that you can truly solve your child care dilemma with the tools you've just acquired.

Please also write to your elected officials and urge their support on child care and work/family legislation. You *can* make a difference.

My best of luck to you—I look forward to hearing from you.

—Sonja Cooper

Resources

NATIONAL ASSOCIATIONS
AND PUBLICATIONS FOR PARENTS
AND OTHER CAREGIVERS

Administration for Children, Youth and Families
Office of Human Development Services
Department of Health and Human Services
200 Independence Avenue, SW
Washington, DC 20201

American Association for Gifted Children
15 Gramercy Park
New York, NY 10003

American Montessori Society
175 Fifth Avenue
New York, NY 10010

Big Brothers/Big Sisters of America
117 South 17th Street, Suite 1200
Philadelphia, PA 19103

Bureau of Education for the Handicapped
U.S. Office of Education
Department of Health and Human Services
7th & D Streets, SW
Washington, DC 20036

Child Care Information Exchange
P.O. Box 2890
Redmond, WA 98052

Child Care Law Project
625 Market Street, Suite 816
San Francisco, CA 94105

Children's Defense Fund
1520 New Hampshire Avenue, NW
Washington, DC 20005

Children's Rights Group
693 Mission Street
San Francisco, CA 94105

Children's Rights, Inc.
3443 17th Street, NW
Washington, DC 20010

Family Service of America
44 East 23rd Street
New York, NY 10010

Food and Nutrition Service
U.S. Department of Agriculture
Alexandria, VA 22302

Foster Grandparents Program
ACTION
806 Connecticut Avenue, NW
Washington, DC 20525

Head Start Bureau
Department of Health and Human Services
P.O. Box 1182
Washington, DC 20013

Infant Stimulation Education Association
UCLA Medical Center
Factor 50942
Los Angeles, CA 90024

International Concerns Committee for Children
911 Cypress Drive
Boulder, CO 80303

National Association for the Education of Young Children
1834 Connecticut Avenue, NW
Washington, DC 20009

National Association for Retarded Citizens (NARC)
2709 Avenue E East
Arlington, TX 76011

National Black Child Development Institute
1463 Rhode Island Avenue, NW
Washington, DC 20005

National Committee for Adoption
2025 M Street, Suite 512
Washington, DC 20036

National Committee for Prevention of Child Abuse
332 South Michigan Avenue, Suite 1250
Chicago, IL 60604

Play Schools Association
120 West 57th Street
New York, NY 10019

Day Care U.S.A. Newsletter
Day Care Information Service
United Communications Group
8701 Georgia Avenue, Suite 800
Silver Springs, MD 20910

Journal of Family Issues
Sage Publications, Inc.
275 South Beverly Drive
Beverly Hills, CA 90212

Parents Magazine
Parents Magazine Enterprises, Inc.
80 New Bridge Road
Bergenfield, NJ 07621

Work/Family Directions
9 Galen Street, Suite 230
Watertown, MA 02172

Working Mother Magazine
Working Woman/McCall's Group
230 Park Avenue
New York, NY 10169

Young Children
Journal of the National Association for the Education
  of Young Children
1834 Connecticut Ave, NW
Washington, DC 20009

State-by-State Resource List

The following entries provide the basic guidelines for child care in each state. "Family Day Care" is defined as day care provided in the home of the caregiver. "Center-Based Day Care" is day care provided at a professional facility. The ratios provided are for the number of qualified care provider's required by law per the number of children in a specific age group. Restrictions and definitions vary from state to state. For more detailed information contact the state agencies or visit their websites.

Alabama

Family and Children's Services
Department of Human Resources
Office of Day Care & Child Development
50 Ripley Street
Montgomery, AL 36130
(334) 242-1425

Family Day Care Ratio:

All ages	1:6

Center-Based:

3 weeks–18 months	1:6
18 months–2½ years	1:8
2½–4 years	1:12
4–6 years	1:20
6–8 years	1:22
8 years and up	1:25

Qualifications:
Child care workers or teachers must be at least 19 years old and have a high school diploma or Graduate Equivalency Degree (GED).

State Home Page:
http://alaweb.asc.edu/

Alaska

Department of Health & Social Services
Division of Family & Youth Services
PO Box 110630
Juneau, AK 99501

Family Day Care Ratio:

All ages, with a maximum of three children under 30 months old, regardless of the ages of the other children	1:8

Center-Based:

Infant	1:5
Toddler	1:6
Preschool	1:10
Kindergarten	1:15
School-age	1:20
Mixed	Follow ratio for the youngest child in the group

Qualifications:
Must be at least 18 years old. Exceptions are allowed for some 14- to 17-year-olds.

State Home Page:
http://www.state.ak.us

Arizona

Department of Health Services
Office of Child Care Licensing
1647 E. Morten, Suite 230
Phoenix, AZ 85020
(602) 255-1272

Family Day Care Ratio:

All ages, serving 5–10 children	1:5
All ages, serving 1–4 children	1:4

Center-Based:

Infant	1:5
1 year	1:6
Preschool	1:10
Kindergarten	1:15
School-age	1:20

Qualifications: Must be at least 18 years old and have a high school diploma and six months' experience, or Childhood Development Associate (CDA) certificate or equivalent, or associate in arts (A.A.) or bachelor's (B.A.) in early childhood education (ECE) or child development or related field.

State Home Page:

http://www.state.az.us

Arkansas

Department of Health
4815 West Mackham Street
Little Rock, AR 72201
(501) 661-2112

Family Day Care Ratio:

Three years and up	1:10

Mixed group with two children
under two years, including preschool
family members   1:7

Center-Based:

Infant   1:6

Toddler   1:9

3 years   1:12

4 years   1:15

5 years   1:18

School-age   1:20

Qualifications:

Must be at least 18 years old with a high school diploma or GED.

State Home Page:

http://www.state.ar.us/

California

Department of Social Services
744 P Street
MS 19-50
Sacramento, CA 95814
(916) 324-4031

Family Day Care Ratio:

All ages, with no more than three
infants, including provider's own
children under 10 years old
(with a maximum of four infants)   1:6

Center-Based:

Infants   1:4

Preschool   1:12

| School-age | 1:14 |
| Mixed group | 1:12 |

Qualifications:
Must be at least 18 years old and have 12 units ECE plus six months' experience, or CDA credential and six months' experience, or hold a current child care center permit.

State Home Page:
http://state.ca.us/

Colorado

Department of Human Services
Division of Child Care Services
1575 Sherman
Denver, CO 80203
(303) 866-5958

Family Day Care Ratio:

All ages, including family members, plus two additional before- and after-school children, with no more than two children under two years, or if provider has been licensed for at least two years with no complaints, three children under two years with no additional before and after school children	1:6
Infant	1:4
Toddler	1:6
Large family day care home, including two children under two years who are siblings of older children	2:12

Center-Based:

| Infant–toddler | 1:5 |

2 years	1:7
2½–3 years	1:8
3 years	1:10
4 years	1:12
5 years and up	1:15

Qualifications:

Must be at least 18 years old and meet one of the following requirements:

❖ 36 months' (5,460 hours) experience
❖ completed a vocational/occupational education sequence in child growth and development with 12 months' experience
❖ completed course of training by the Department of Human Services
❖ 12 semester hours of college-level courses in child growth and development and/or early childhood education and nine months' experience
❖ two years college with at least one college course in child development and six months' experience
❖ CDA, CCP or other Department-approved credential or two-year or bachelor's degree in child development or early childhood education

State Home Page:

http://www.state.co.us/

Connecticut

Department of Public Health
Child Day Care Licensing
410 Capitol Avenue
MS 12 DAC
PO Box 340308
Hartford, CT 06134-0308
(860) 509-8045

Family Day Care Ratio:

All ages, including provider's
children not in school full time,

with a maximum of two infants
per provider, in addition to six
full-time children; may have
up to three school-age children for
up to three hours before and after
school, during the school year only   1:6

Center-Based:

Infants   1:4

Toddlers   1:4

Preschool over 3 years   1:10

School-age   1:10

Mixed group   1:4

Qualifications:

Teachers in charge of a group must be at least 18 years old and have a high school diploma or GED or 540 hours' documented experience with the applicable age group.

State Home Page:

http://www.state.ct.us/

Delaware

Department of Services for Children Youth & Families
Office of Child Care Licensing
1825 Faulkland Road
Wilmington, DE 19805
(302) 892-5800

Family Day Care Ratio:

Infant–preschool, with a
maximum of three children under
two years and two children under
12 months   1:4

Infant–preschool, with two
additional school-age children

for a Level I provider, including family members under school age	1:4
Infant–preschool, with a maximum of three children under two years and two children under 12 months	1:6
Infant–preschool, with three additional school-age children for a Level II provider, including family members under school age	1:6

Center-Based:

Infants	1:4
12–24 months	1:7
2–3 years	1:10
3–4 years	1:12
4–5 years	1:15
5 years and up	1:25
Mixed groups	For children under 24 months, follow the ratio for the youngest child in the group For groups including children over 24 months, follow the ratio for the age group with the largest number of children present

Qualifications:

Must be at least 18 years old and meet one of the following requirements:

- ❖ have a four-year degree with at least three credit hours in child development or early childhood education and three months supervised student teaching or six months experience working with children in a group setting
- ❖ an associate degree with three credit hours in child development or early childhood education and six months' experience
- ❖ a CDA with six months' experience

- ❖ a high school diploma with successful completion of vocational child care program or a one year certificate program in child development or early childhood education and one year's experience
- ❖ high school diploma or equivalent and 60 clock hours of training in child development or early childhood education and one year's experience

For more information, call 800-598-KIDS.

State Home Page:
http://www.state/de.us/

District of Columbia

Division of Consumer and Regulatory Affairs
Child Care Branch
614 H Street, NW, Rm. 1035
Washington, DC 20001
(202) 727-7226

Family Child Care Ratio:

All ages, including family members under six years	1:5
Infants	1:2

Center-Based:

2–2½ years	1:4
2½ years–3 years	1:8
4 years	1:10
5 years	1:15
6–14 years	1:15
Mixed group	Ratio shall be adjusted to protect the welfare of the younger children

Qualifications:

Teachers must be at least 18 years old and meet one of the following requirements:

❖ a bachelor's degree in early childhood education or a related field, including a minimum of 15 hours in early childhood education courses

❖ two or more years of college, including a minimum of 15 hours in early childhood education courses and one year's experience in a child development facility

❖ a high school diploma or equivalent and three years' experience as a teacher or assistant teacher in a child development center

❖ experience as a teacher or assistant teacher in a licensed child development center with a CDA

State Home Page:

http://www.ci.washington.dc.us/

Florida

Department of Children and Families
2811-A Industrial Plaza Drive
Tallahassee, FL 32301
(904) 488-4900

Family Day Care Ratio:

A family day care home is allowed to provide care for one of the following groups of children, including those children under 13 years who are related to the caregiver:

Infant–1 year	1:4
1 year–preschool	1:6
Mixed group with a maximum of three children infant to one year	1:6
Mixed group with a maximum of five preschool, and of those five no more than two under one year	1:10

Center-Based:

Infant–1 year	1:4
1–2 years	1:6
2–3 years	1:11
3–4 years	1:15
4–5 years	1:20
School-age	1:25
Mixed group	1:4 for groups including infants under one year
	1:6 for groups including infants over one year
	Ratio for groups not including infants should follow the ratio for the age of the majority of the children in the group

Qualifications:

Caregivers in charge of a group must be at least 18 years old and must complete the Department of Health and Rehabilitative Services approved introductory training course.

State Home Page:

http://www.state.fl.us/

Georgia

Department of Human Resources
Child Care Licensing Section
2 Peachtree Street NW, 32nd Floor
Atlanta, GA 30303
(404) 657-5562

Family Day Care Ratio:

Infants, if no more than three children are under 12 months	1:3

All ages, with a maximum of six unrelated children plus two additional children three years and up for two hours per day	1:6
All ages, if more than six children are under three years	2:6
All ages, if more than eight children are under five years	2:8

Center-Based:

Infants, if not walking	1:6
1 year (if walking)	1:8
2 years	1:10
3 years	1:15
4 years	1:18
5 years	1:20
School-age	1:25
Mixed group	Follow ratio for the youngest child in the group if 20 percent or more are present

Qualifications:

Teachers/Lead Caregivers must be at least 18 years old and have a high school diploma, GED or one year's experience.

State Home Page:

http://www.state.ga.us/

Hawaii

Department of Human Services
Self-Sufficiency and Support Services Department
1001 Bishop Street
Pacific Tower, Suite 900
Honolulu, HI 96813
(808) 586-5770

Family Day Ratio:

All ages, with no more than two
under 18 months, including
provider's own children,
unless they are in school or
enrolled in a child care facility
for more than six hours per day   1:6

Center-Based Ratio:

Infants	1:3
Toddlers	1:4
2 years	1:8
3 years	1:12
4 years	1:16
School-age	1:20
Mixed group	Follow ratio for age of youngest child

Qualifications: Must be at least 18 years old and meet one of the following requirements:

- ❖ a degree in child development or early childhood education and six months' working experience
- ❖ a postsecondary credential in a child development associate program
- ❖ a two-year (60 credit) college program with a certificate in early childhood education plus one year's experience
- ❖ a baccalaureate in elementary education plus six months' work experience in an early childhood program plus six credits of approved child development or early childhood education training courses
- ❖ a baccalaureate in any field plus six months' work in early childhood program plus 12 credits of approved child development or early childhood courses

State Home Page:

http://www.state.hi.us/

Idaho

Department of Health and Welfare
Bureau of Family and Children's Services
450 W. State Street
PO Box 83720
Boise, ID 93720
(208) 334-5691

Family Day Care Ratio:

All ages	1:6

Center-Based:

All ages	1:12

Qualifications:

Center staff requires four hours' annual training

State Home Page:

http://www.state.id.us/

Illinois

Department of Children and Family Services
406 E. Monroe Street, #60
Springfield, IL 62701
(217) 785-2688

Family Day Care Ratio:

All ages, with no more than five children under five years and no more than three children under two years, including the provider's own children under 12 years	1:12
All ages, with six children under five years and no children under three years	1:12
School-age	1:8

Center-Based:

Infants	1:4
Toddlers	1:5
2 years	1:8
Preschool	1:10
School-age	1:20
Mixed group	Follow the ratio for the age of the youngest child in the group

Qualifications:

Must be at least 19 years old and have a high school diploma or equivalent and two years' full-time experience in a field related to programming for young children or two years' college credit, including six semester hours in courses directly related to child care and/or child development (birth to six years) or one year's (1,560 clock hours) child development experience in a nursery school, kindergarten or licensed day care center and one year of college credits, including six semester hours in courses directly related to child care and/or child development or a CDA credential.

State Home Page:

http://www.state.il.us/

Indiana

Department of Family & Social Services
Day Care Licensing Unit
402 W. Washington Street, Rm. W364
Indianapolis, IN 46204
(317) 232-4442

Family Day Care Ratio:

The maximum capacity of a child care home is 1:12 plus three children during the school year who are enrolled at least in grade 1.

Infant–2 years, with less than two children at least 16 months and walking	1:4

Infant–2 years, with at least two children at least 16 months and walking	1:6
Infant–6 years, with no more than three children under 16 months of age and must be walking	1:10
3–10 years	1:12
All ages	1:12

Center-Based:

Infants	1:4
Toddlers	1:5
2 years	1:5
3 years	1:10
4 years	1:12
5 years	1:15
6 years and up	1:20

Qualifications:

Must be at least 18 years old (21 if working with infants) and have a high school diploma or equivalent.

State Home Page:

http://www.state.in.us/

Iowa

Iowa Department of Human Services
Child Care Licensing
Hoover State Office Building
5th Floor
Des Moines, IA 50319
(515) 281-6074

Family Day Care Ratio:

All ages, including provider's preschool children and with no more than four children under two years	1:6

Center-Based:

Infants	1:4
2 years	1:6
3 years	1:8
4 years	1:12
5–10 years	1:15
Mixed group	Follow ratio for the age of the youngest child in the group

Qualifications:

Must be at least 16 years old.

State Home Page:

http://www.state.ia.us/

Kansas

Department of Health and Environment
Child Care Licensing
109 SW 9th Street
Mills Bldg., 400-C
Topeka, KS 66612
(913) 296-1272

Family Day Care Ratios:

Birth–18 months	1:3

Center-Based:

Infants	1:3
Toddlers	1:5

2½–6 years	1:10
3–6 years	1:12
School-age (K–6th)	1:14
School-age (6th–12th)	1:16
Mixed group (0–6 years), with a maximum of eight children in one group	1:4

Qualifications:

Group leader for fewer than 13 children must be at least 18 years old with a high school diploma or equivalent plus six months' teaching experience or five sessions of 2½ hours of observation in a child care facility with children of same age plus 10 hours of approved workshops or three semester hours academic credit or equivalent training in child development, early childhood education, curriculum resources plus supervised observation in high school or college or three months work experience or CDA.

Group leader for 13 to 24 must be at least 18 years old with a high school diploma or equivalent plus five sessions of observation and one year teaching experience or one year supervised practicum or seven to nine semester hours academic credit or equivalent training in child development or early childhood education plus three months teaching experience or one year supervised practicum or CDA.

State Home Page:

http://www.state.ks.us/

Kentucky

Cabinet for Health Services
Cabinet for Human Resources Bldg.
OIG Division of Licensing & Regulations
275 East Main Street, 4th Floor East A
Frankfort, KY 40621
(502) 564-2800

Family Day Care Ratio:

In any group if more than four infants are in care, the provider shall employ an assistant who must be 16 years of age.

Infant–6 years, including provider's own or related children	1:6
6 years and up	1:10

Center Based:

Infants	1:5
Toddlers	1:6
2–3 years	1:10
3–4 years	1:12
4–5 years	1:14
School-age	1:15
7 years and up (before/after school)	1:25
7 years and up (full-time care)	1:20

Qualifications:

Must be at least 18 years old.

State Home Page:

http://www.state.ky.us/

Louisiana

Department of Social Services
Bureau of Licensing
PO Box 3078
Baton Rouge, LA 70821
(504) 922-0015

Family Day Care Ratio:

All ages	1:6

Center-Based:

Birth–1 year	1:6

1–2 years	1:8
2–3 years	1:12
3–4 years	1:14
4–5 years	1:16
5–6 years	1:20
School-age	1:25
Mixed group	Observe average ratio as long as no children under two years are present

Qualifications:
Staff must be at least 18-years old

State Home Page:
http://www.state.la.us/

Maine

Bureau of Child & Family Services
Maine Division of Licensing, ACL
221 State Street State House, Station 11
Augusta, ME 04333
(207) 287-5060

Family Day Care Ratio:

Birth–2 years	1:4
2 years–school-age, plus two school-age children	1:8
School-age	1:12
Mixed group	No more than three under two years with a maximum of six plus two school-age children

Center-Based:

Infants	1:4

Toddlers	1:5
2½–3 years	1:8
3–6 years	1:10
School-age	1:10
Mixed group	Follow ratio for the age of the youngest child in the group

Qualifications:

Head teacher or family day care provider for fewer than 13 children, must be at least 18 years old and have six hours' training in child care or early childhood education.

Head teacher for 13 to 24 children, must be at least 21 years old with a high school diploma or equivalent and have 12 months' employment in licensed child day care facility for 13 or more children; or 12 months' experience as an operator of a program for three to 12 children (including as a family day care provider) and have six hours' training in child care or early childhood education topics; or have one year of (30 credit hours) college courses, including six hours in field closely related to caring for children and six months' experience or CDA.

Group Leader must be at least 18 years old and have a CDA or six months' working experience with a group of 13 or more children; or have one year (30 credits) college work in a child-related field.

State Home Page:

http://www.state.me.us/

Maryland

Department of Human Resources
Child Care Administration
311 W. Saratoga Street, First Floor
Baltimore, MD 21201
(410) 767-7798

Family Day Care Ratio:

All ages, with no more than two children under two years	1:8

Center-Based:

Infants	1:3
Young toddlers	1:3
2 years	1:6
Preschool	1:10
School-age	1:15
Mixed group	Varies by ages

Qualifications:

Senior staff must be at least 24 years old, with a high school diploma or equivalent or successful completion of courses for credit from accredited college or university and six semester hours or 90 clock hours of approved training or CDA and either one year supervised work experience in group program for preschoolers or as a registered family child care provider or one year of college or equivalent combination of college and experience; or must be at least 19 years and hold an A.A. degree in early childhood education or recreation. Persons approved or certified by State Department of Education as teacher for grades nursery through third grade are also considered qualified as senior staff.

State Home Page:

http://www.mec.state.md.us/

Massachusetts

Office for Children
One Ashburton Place, Rm. 111
Boston, MA 02108
(627) 727-8900

Family Day Care Ratio:

Infants, with minimum of one at least 15 months and walking	1:3
Under seven years, including children living in the home	1:6

Center-Based:

Infants	1:3 / 2:4–7
Toddlers	1:4 / 2:5–9
Preschool (full-day)	1:10
Preschool (half-day)	1:12
School-age	1:13
Mixed group (infants–33 months)	1:5
Mixed group (33 months–7 years)	1:7

Qualifications:

Must be at least 21 years old or have a high school diploma or equivalent and meet one of the following requirements:

- at least nine months of supervised work experience with children under seven years old and have a three-credit course in child growth and development
- an associate or advanced degree in early childhood education or related field and three months' required work experience
- a bachelor's degree in an unrelated field, six months' required work experience and a three-credit course in child growth and development.

To be considered an infant/toddler teacher, the required work experience includes time working with that age group.

State Home Page:

http://www.state.ma.us/

Michigan

Department of Consumer & Industry Services
Bureau of Regulatory Services
Division of Child Day Care Licensing
7109 W. Saginaw, 2nd Floor
PO Box 30650
Lansing, MI 48909
(517) 373-8300

Family Day Care Ratio:

All ages, with no more than four
children under 30 months and
no more than two of those under
18 months, including family
members under seven years   1:16

Center-Based:

Infants, up to 30 months	1:4
2½–3 years	1:10
4–5 years	1:12
6–12 years	1:20
13–17 years	1:30
Mixed group	Follow ratio for the age of the youngest child in the group

Qualifications:

None specified except for program director.

State Home Page:

http://info.migov.state.mi.us/

Minnesota

Department of Human Services
Division of Licensing
444 Lafayette Road
St. Paul, MN 55155
(612) 296-3971

Family Day Care Ratio:

Minnesota has seven classes of family day care, each with different ratios
and requirements. Please contact the licensing agency above for more
information.

Center-Based:

Infants   1:4

Toddlers	1:7
Preschool	1:10
School-age	1:15
Mixed group	Follow ratio for age of the youngest child in group

Qualifications:

Extensive requirements, please contact licensing agency for details.

State Home Page:

http://state.mn.us/

Mississippi

Department of Health
Division of Child Care
PO Box 1700
Jackson, MS 39215
(601) 960-7613

Family Day Care Ratio:

All ages	1:5

Center-Based:

Birth–11 months	1:5
1 year	1:9
2 years	1:12
3 years	1:14
4 years	1:16
5 years–9	1:20
10–12 years	1:25
Mixed group	Follow ratio for age of the youngest child in group

Qualifications:

Caregiver must be at least 18 years old and hold a high school diploma or GED or have a CDA credential or three years' prior experience as a caregiver or caregiver's assistant.

State Home Page:

http://state.ms.us

Missouri

Division of Health
Bureau of Child Care, Safety and Licensure
PO Box 570
Jefferson City, MO 65102
(573) 751-2450

Family Day Care Ratio:

Infants	1:4
All ages (ages of children determine necessity of an assistant)	1:10

Center-Based:

Infants	1:4
Toddlers	1:8
Preschool	1:10
School-age	1:16

Qualifications:

Must be at least 18 years old and meet general health requirements.

State Home Page:

http://www.state.mo.us

Montana

Public Health & Human Services
Department of Child Care
PO Box 8005
Helena, MT 59604
(406) 444–5900

Family Day Care Ratio:

All ages, including provider's children who are under six years	1:16

Center-Based:

Infants	1:4
Toddlers	1:8
Preschool	1:10
School-age	1:14

Qualifications:

Primary caregiver must be at least 18 years old and have two years' experience as a licensed/registered family day care home provider or day care center staff or have a B.A. in education or a related field. Must also have sufficient language skills and complete a minimum of eight hours of specified training in the first year of employment.

State Home Page:

http://www.mt.gov

Nebraska

Health & Human Services Agency
Resource Development & Support Unit
PO Box 95044
Lincoln, NE 68509
(402) 471-9431

Family Day Care Ratio:

Infants	1:4

All ages, including provider's own children, with no more than two children under 18 months and two additional children during non-school hours 1:8

Mixed group, with no more than two infants at one time 1:8

School-age 1:10

Center-Based:

Infants	1:4
Toddlers	1:6
Preschool (3 years)	1:10
Preschool (4–5 years)	1:12
School-age	1:15
Mixed group	Center-wide ratio count

Qualifications:

Staff must be "legal age of majority" and meet one of the following requirements:

❖ a written, department-approved plan to acquire at least three credit hours or 15 clock hours of department-approved in-service training in child development/early childhood education or child care administration within 12 months of hiring
❖ or a CDA
❖ or a bachelor's or associate's degree in a field related to care and education of children ages birth to 12 years (e.g., early childhood education, child development, elementary education or special education)
❖ or one year verified group experience with a positive reference from a supervisor

State Home Page:

http://www.state.ne.us/

Nevada

Bureau of Services for Child Care
Child Care Licensing
3920 E. Idaho Street
Elko, NV 89801
(702) 753-1237

Family Day Care Ratio:

All ages, not including provider's
family members with a maximum
of four children under two years and
no more than two children under
one year   1:6

Center-Based:

Varies depending on age of children. Whenever one or more infants or
toddlers are being cared for in a child care center, the licensee must have
at least one caretaker on duty who is designated to provide that care.

Qualifications:

Caretaker must be at least 16 years old and have completed, or be
currently enrolled in, an approved course in the development of children.
Must complete a course of training in child care within six months of
employment unless such a course was completed within the previous 12
months.

State Home Page:

http://www.state.nv.us/

New Hampshire

Division of Public Health Services
Bureau of Child Care Licensing
6 Hazen Drive
Concord, NH 03301
(603) 271-4624

Family Day Care Ratios:

One provider may care for any one of the following groups of children, including the provider's own biological or adopted children, foster and resident children up to 10 years:

- ❖ six preschool children and three school-age children with no more than three children under 36 months, of which no more than two shall be under 19 months
- ❖ five preschool children and three school-age children with no more than four children under 36 months, of which no more than two children shall be under 24 months
- ❖ four children under 36 months
- ❖ six preschool children and three school-age children with no more than four children under 36 months (assistant or aid required)

Center-Based:

6 weeks–12 months	1:4
13–24 months	1:5
25–35 months	1:6
36–47 months	1:8
48–59 months	1:12
60 months and up	1:15
Mixed groups	Ratio based on the average age of the group

Qualifications:

Teacher must have a high school diploma and meet one of the following requirements:

- ❖ 12 college credits in early childhood education, including three credits in human growth and development
- ❖ minimum of three calendar years of at least 20 hours/week supervised child care experience with a written recommendation from supervisor and six college credits in early childhood education or human growth and development
- ❖ 144 hours of workshops, courses or in-service training with at least 36 hours in growth and development and the remainder in early childhood education

- ❖ employment on July 20, 1990 as a teacher in a facility licensed by the state of New Hampshire and five years' experience as a teacher

State Home Page:

http://www.state.nh.us/

New Jersey

Department of Human Services
Division of Youth and Family Services
Bureau of Licensing
PO Box 717
Trenton, NJ 08625
(609) 292-1018

Family Day Care Ratios:

Infants	1:3
Preschool and up, with three additional children allowed if they reside in the home or are the children of the assistant or substitute	1:5

Center-Based:

Birth–18 months	1:4
18 months–2½ years	1:7
2½–4 years	1:10
4–5 years	1:15
6 years and school-age	1:18

Qualifications:

Group teacher must have an associate degree in early childhood education or child development; or 15 college credits, including at least six in early childhood education or child development with the remainder from education, psychology, health care, nursing or other fields related to child growth and development; or credential as a CDA or as a Recreation Technician from National Recreation Professionals Association (NRPA).

State Home Page:

http://www.state.nj.us/

New Mexico

Children Youth and Families Department
Licensing & Certification Bureau
PERA Bldg. Rm. 121
PO Drawer 5160
Santa Fe, NM 87502
(505) 827-4118 or 4185

Family Day Care Ratio:

All ages, including provider's own children under six years	1:6
With no more than two children under two years, including provider's own children under six years	2:7–12

Center-Based:

Infants	1:6
Toddlers	1:6
Preschool	1:12
School-age	1:15
Mixed group	Same as above

Qualifications:

Staff must be at least 18 years old

State Home Page:

http://www.state.nm.us

New York

New York State Department of Social Services
Bureau of Early Childhood Services

40 N. Pearl Street, 11-B
Albany, NY 12243
(518) 474-9454

Family Day Care Ratio:

Standard ratio is 1:6.

For children six weeks–12 years, no more than two children under the age of two years; no more than five children if any child present is under age two; up to two additional school-age children may be cared for with Department approval following an on-site visit.

For group family child care, no more than four children under the age of two years; no more than six children under the age of three years; no more than 10 children if any child present is under age two; up to two additional school-age children may be cared for with Department approval following an on-site visit.

Center-Based:

6 weeks–1½ years	1:4
1½–3 years	1:5
3 years	1:7
4 years	1:8
5 years	1:9
6–10 years	1:10
10–12 years	1:15

Qualifications:

Heads of groups must have one of the following:
- ❖ an A.A. in early childhood education, child development or another child-related area
- ❖ CDA credential and two years' experience related to caring for children
- ❖ a high school diploma or equivalent and three years' experience

Additionally, if caring for a group of children under the age of three years, head must also have one year's experience and/or training specifically in infant and toddler care.

State Home Page:

http://www.state.ny.us

North Carolina

Division of Child Development
Child Day Care Section
PO Box 29553
Raleigh, NC 27626
(919) 662-4499

Family Day Care Ratio:

Infants and preschool	1:5

May also care for three additional school-age children; maximum of eight children at any one time, including provider's own preschool children.

Center-Based:

Birth–1 year	1:5
1–2 years	1:6
2 years	1:10
3–4 years	1:15
4–5 years	1:20
5 years	1:25

Qualifications:

Staff must be at least 18 years old and meet general health requirements.

State Home Page:

http://www.state.nc.us/DHR/DCD

North Dakota

North Dakota Department of Human Services
Children and Family Services
State Capitol Building

600 E. Boulevard Avenue
Bismarck, ND 58505
(701) 328-4809

Family Day Care Ratio:

All ages, with two additional school-age children before and after school	1:7

Center-Based:

Birth–2 years	1:4
2 years	1:5
3 years	1:7
4 years	1:10
5 years	1:12
6–12 years	1:18

Qualifications:

Child care supervisor must have training and demonstrated ability to work with young children and have at least one of the following:

* A.A. in early childhood development
* CDA or similar local, state, or federal certification
* Montessori teacher certification
* high school diploma and one year's experience in child care or a similar setting
* high school equivalency and one year experience in child care or a similar setting

State Home Page:

http://www.state.nd.us/

Ohio

Ohio Department of Human Services
Bureau of Child Care Services
Child Day Care Licensing Section

65 E. State Street, 5th Floor
Columbus, OH 43215
(614) 466-3822

Family Day Care Ratio:

All ages, including provider's own children under six years, with no more than three children under two years	1:6

Center-Based:

Infants, birth–12 months	1:5
Infants, 12–17 months	1:6
Toddlers, 18–29 months	1:7
Toddlers, 30–35 months	1:8
Preschool, 3 years	1:12
Preschool, 4–5 years	1:14
School-age to 10 years	1:18
School-age, 11–14 years	1:20
Mixed group	Follow ratio for the age of the youngest child in the group

Qualifications:

Child care staff member must be at least 18 years old and have a high school education and have completed a training program approved by the Department of Human Services. Such approved programs include a vocational education home economics course or a child care job training program for adults that must include completing five required and three elective courses for a total of 160 contact hours.

State Home Page:

http://www.state.oh.us/

Oklahoma

Department of Human Services
Office of Child Care
4545 N. Lincoln, Suite 100
PO Box 25352
Oklahoma City, OK 73105
(405) 521-3561

Family Day Care Ratio:

Provider may care for:

- ❖ maximum of seven children, including the provider's own children under five years and not more than two children under age two years
- ❖ maximum of six children with three under age two
- ❖ maximum of five children with four or five under the age of two years

Center-Based:

Birth–9 months	1:4, with a maximum group size of 8
10–23 months	1:6, with a maximum group size of 12
2 years	1:8, with a maximum group size of 16
3 years	1:12, with a maximum group size of 24
4–5 years	1:15, with a maximum group size of 30
6 years and up	1:20, with a maximum group size of 40

Qualifications:

Teachers must be at least 18 years old and have a high school diploma or GED or be in the process of receiving a GED.

State Home Page:

http://www.state.ok.us/

Oregon

Employment Department
Child Care Division
875 Union Street, NE
Salem, OR 97311
(503) 378-3178

Family Day Care Ratio:

All ages with six preschool
and four school-age children,
including the provider's own
children (restrictions also apply
to ages of preschool children)   1:10

Center-Based:

Infants	1:4
Toddlers	1:4
Preschool	1:10
School-age	1:15
Mixed group	Follow ratio for the age of the youngest child in the group

Qualifications:

Teachers must be at least 18 years old and have one of the following

- ❖ 20 semester hours of training in a college or university in early childhood education, child development or special education
- ❖ a child development associate credential
- ❖ at least one year of successful full-time work in a group program for children

State Home Page:

http://www.state.or.us/

Pennsylvania

Department of Public Welfare
Bureau of Child Day Care Services

Office of Children Youth and Family Services
Complex 3, 4th Floor
PO Box 2675
Harrisburg, PA 17105
(717) 787-8691

Family Day Care Ratio:

All ages, with no more than two infants and no more than five may be a combination of infants and toddlers	1:6

Center-Based:

Infants	1:4
Young toddlers	1:5
Older toddlers	1:6
Preschool	1:10
Young school-age	1:12
Older school-age	1:15
Mixed group	Follow ratio for the age of the youngest child in the group

Qualifications:

Staff must be at least 18 years old and have a CDA credential or equivalent, such as 15 credits from an accredited college or university in early childhood education or child development and one year's experience or 30 credits from an accredited college or university in early childhood education or child development.

State Home Page:

http://www.state.pa.us/

Rhode Island

Department for Children Youth and Families
Day Care Licensing, Bldg. 3
610 Mount Pleasant Avenue

Providence, RI 02908
(401) 277-4741

Family Day Care Ratio:
If care is provided to child under 18 months of age, care for no more than four children under six years, no more than two of which can be under the age of 18 months; providers may have up to eight children if there is an approved assistant; no more than four may be under 18 months old.

Center-Based:

Infants	1:4
Toddlers	1:6
3 years	1:9
4 years	1:10
5 years	1:12
School-age	1:13
Mixed group	Follow the ratio for the age of the youngest child in the group

Qualifications:
Teacher must have a current Rhode Island certificate in early childhood education or a bachelor's or master's degree in early childhood education from an accredited or approved school and a minimum of three months' supervised teaching experience in a licensed or approved early childhood program (which may be a student teaching experience) or a bachelor's degree from an accredited or approved school and required course work and experience defined in Rhode Island Early Childhood Certification standards.

State Home Page:
http://www.state.ri.us/

South Carolina

South Carolina Department of Social Services
PO Box 1520

Columbia, SC 29202
(803) 734-5740

Family Day Care Ratio:

All ages, including provider's family members under 12 years	1:6

Center-Based:

Infants	1:6
1–2 years	1:6
2–3 years	1:10
3–4 years	1:14
4–5 years	1:19
5–6 years	1:22
6–12 years	1:24
Mixed group	As indicated

Qualifications:

Staff must be at least 18 years old and able to read and write. Must have a high school diploma or GED and at least six months' experience as a caregiver in a licensed/approved facility and have completed six hours of training in child growth and development/early childhood education within six months of hiring.

State Home Page:

http://www.state.sc.us/

South Dakota

Department of Social Services—Child Care Services
Richard F. Kreip Building
700 Governor's Drive
Pierre, SD 57501
(605) 773-4766

Family Day Care Ratio:

All ages, with no more than four
under two years and no more than
two of those four under one year,
including provider's own children
under six years   1:12

Center-Based:

Infants   1:5

Toddlers (up to 3 years)   1:5

Preschool (3–6 years)   1:10

School-age   1:15

Mixed group   According to number in each
                                        group

Qualifications:

Teacher must be at least 18 years old and have one of the following:

- a bachelor's in fields of education or human development and at least two years' experience in child care
- a bachelor's in elementary education and at least two years' experience in child care
- a bachelor's in elementary education if working only with school-age children
- a bachelor's in early childhood education or an associate's in early childhood development or certification as a child development associate, or certification in Montessori teacher training program and at least one year's experience in a Montessori school or child care setting
- a child development technician diploma
- at least five years' supervised experience in a child care center
- a pre-kindergarten teacher endorsement

State Home Page:

http://www.state.sd.us/

Tennessee

Department of Human Services
Day Care Licensing Unit
Citizens Plaza
400 Deaderick Street
Nashville, TN 37248
(615) 313-4778

Family Day Care Ratio:

All ages, with no more than four children under two years, including children under nine related to the provider	1:7

Center-Based:

Infants	1:5
Toddlers	1:7
2 years	1:8
3 years	1:10
4 years	1:15
5 years	1:20
School-age	1:25
Mixed group	Ranges from 1:6 for infants/toddlers to 1:20 for 4–5 years

Qualifications:

Caregivers must be at least 18 years old and able to read and write, have a high school diploma or equivalent.

State Home Page:

http://www.state.tn.us/

Texas

Texas Department of Protective and Regulatory Services
Child Care Licensing
PO Box 149030, MCE-550
Austin, TX 78714
(512) 438-3269

Family Day Care Ratio:

Preschool, plus six school-age children under 14 years, including the provider's own children	1:6

Center-Based:

Birth–12 months	1:4 / 2:10
13–17 months	1:5 / 2:12
18–23 months	1:7 / 2:15
2 years	1:9 / 2:18
3 years	1:13 / 2:26
4 years	1:16 / 2:28
5 years	1:20 / 2:30
6–8 years	1:22 / 2:35
9–13 years	1:25 / 2:35

Qualifications:

Staff must be at least 18 years old and have a high school diploma or equivalent.

State Home Page:

http://www.state.tx.us/

Utah

Bureau of Licensing, Child Care Unit
PO Box 142853

Salt Lake City, UT 84114
(801) 538-6152

Family Day Care Ratio:

Infants	1:3
All ages, with no more than two children under two years	1:6

If all children are two and older, then six children plus two school-age children may be cared for, but if one child is under age two, then six children plus one school-age child may be cared for. All ratios include the caregiver's own children under age six and those who have not completed kindergarten.

Center-Based:

Infants	1:4
Toddlers under 2 years	1:4
2 years	1:7
3 years	1:12
4 years	1:15
5 years	1:20

Qualifications:

Caregivers and group leaders must be at least 18 years old with a high school diploma or GED.

State Home Page:

http://www.state.ut.us/

Vermont

Department of Social and Rehabilitative Services
Child Care Services Division
Licensing Unit
103 South Main Street
Waterbury, VT 05671
(802) 241-2158

Family Day Care Ratio:

Infants, including provider's own children under two years	1:2
All ages plus additional four school-age children for not more than four hours per day on a before- and/or after-school basis, not including provider's own children over two years	1:6

Center-Based:

Infants	1:4
Toddlers	1:5
Preschool	1:10
School-age	1:13
Mixed group	Follow lowest ratio

Qualifications:

Staff must be at least 18 years old (17 years old if a vo-tech child care student or graduate) and have a CDA or CCP credential or an associate degree in early childhood or human/child development or one year's successful experience working with young children and one higher education course in early childhood education or human/child development.

State Home Page:

http://www.state.vt.us/

Virginia

Department of Social Services
Division of Licensing Programs
730 E. Broad Street
Theater Row Bldg.
Richmond, VA 23219
(804) 692-1787

Family Day Care Ratio:

Birth–15 months	1:4
16–23 months	1:5
2–4 years	1:8
School-age	1:16

Center-Based:

Infants	1:4
Young toddlers	1:5
2–3 years	1:10
4 years	1:12
School-age	1:20
Mixed group	Follow ratio for the age of the youngest child in the group

Qualifications:

Program leaders must be at least 18 years old and have a high school diploma or GED. Must also have one of the following:

- ❖ an endorsement or B.A. in a child-related field
- ❖ 48 semester hours from accredited college or university, at least 12 of which are in a subject relating to group care of children, and six months of age-appropriate program experience
- ❖ a one-year early childhood certificate from an accredited college or university of at least 30 semester hours and six months of age appropriate program experience in group care and participation in a staff training plan of at least 10 hours in the first year of employment

State Home Page:

http://state.va.us/

Washington

Washington Department of Social and Health Services
Office of Child Care Policy
PO Box 45700

Olympia, WA 98504
(360) 902-8038

Family Day Care Ratio:

Providers may care for up to 12 children with a qualified assistant; provider with one year of experience may care for 10 children alone if none are under five years of age; provider with two years of experience, an ECE course and an assistant may care for a maximum of four children under two years of age. May have up to 12 children, including provider's own children. Must be two providers when there are more than two children under age of two; seven or more children are in care and any child is under age two; or, more than 10 children of any age.

Center-Based:

Infants	1:4
Toddlers	1:7
Preschool	1:10
School-age	1:15
Mixed group	Follow ratio for the age of the youngest child in the group

Qualifications:

Child care staff must be 18 years old or older and have a high school education or equivalent or child development knowledge and experience.

State Home Page:

http://www.state.wa.us/

West Virginia

West Virginia Department of Health & Human Services
Day Care Licensing
Capitol Complex, Bldg. 6, Rm. 850-B
1900 Washington Street East
Charleston, WV 25305
(304) 558-7980

Family Day Care Ratio:

All ages, including the provider's own children whether related by blood, marriage or adoption, who live in the home and are under six years, with no more than two children under 24 months allowed at any time   1:6

Center-Based:

Birth–2 years	1:4
2–3 years	1:8
3–4 years	1:10
4–5 years	1:12
5–6 years	1:15
School-age	1:16

Qualifications:

Staff must be at least 18 years old and have a high school education or certified equivalent. Must be able to read and write.

State Home Page:

http://www.state.wv/us/

Wisconsin

Department of Health and Social Services
Division of Children and Family Services
Bureau of Regulation & Licensing
PO Box 8916
Madison, WI 53708
(608) 266-9314

Family Day Care Ratio:

Birth–seven years, but if three or four children are under two years, the

number of other children in
care is reduced   1:8

Center-Based:

Infants	1:4
Toddlers	1:4
2–2½ years	1:6
2½ years–3 years	1:8
3–4 years	1:10
4–5 years	1:17
6 years and up	1:18

Qualifications:

Child care teacher must be at least 18 years old and have high school diploma or equivalent or certificate, credentials or diploma from a postsecondary early childhood training program approved by the Department. Must have 120 days' half-time or 80 days' full-time experience in direct care or certification by the Wisconsin Department of Public Instruction as a nursery school teacher or as an exceptional education needs teacher (or be able to show evidence of meeting the qualifications for certification) and two years documented credit in an institution of higher education with at least three credits or equivalent in early childhood education or satisfactory completion of 80 hours of Department-approved training in early childhood education, CDA credentials or satisfactory completion of another Department-approved competency program.

State Home Page:

http://www.state.wi.us/

Wyoming

Department of Family Services
Division of Juvenile Services
2300 Capitol Avenue, Rm. 323
Cheyenne, WY 82002
(307) 777-6285

Family Day Care Ratio:

All ages, including provider's own preschool children (infant care is limited to two unless another adult is present, then infant capacity can be increased to five)	1:6

Center-Based:

Birth–2 years	1:5
2–3 years	1:8
3–4 years	1:10
4–5 years	1:15
5–6 years	1:20
6 years and up	1:25
Mixed group	Follow ratio for the ages of the youngest child in the group

Qualifications:

Group day care providers must be at least 19 years old and have a high school diploma or GED certificate or six months' documented prior work experience in day care or five clock hours of day care training or a professional credential from a nationally recognized organization.

State Home Page:

http://www.state.wy.us/

Safe Child Care and New Technology

PAY ATTENTION TO YOUR NAGGING FEELINGS

It's 10:30 in the morning and you can't keep your mind on the staff meeting. You picture your baby, 15 miles away, taking her morning nap. You go over your mental checklist again and realize that you've done all the right things before hiring an in-home child care provider: lots of research, checked references and even spent three days at home with them so your baby could get used to the new person with you there. So why is it so hard to relax and "let things work," as your husband says? He thinks you are overreacting and you can't talk to your mother because she thinks you should be at home.

Yesterday, you came home earlier than usual and could have sworn you smelled cigarette smoke (a clear violation of the employment contract). There's a nagging feeling that something just isn't right, but you can't put your finger on it.

What Now?

As more and more parents work outside the home, it's understandable why *safe* child care is a major concern. This trend has not been lost on the business world. Several services take advantage of new technology to meet the needs of parents who want to go the extra mile before and after hiring an in-home provider. They offer everything from pre-employment background checks to hidden surveillance cameras. It can be costly, but peace of mind doesn't come cheap.

TrustLine

Mary Beth Phillips's daughter was permanently blinded after being shaken as a six-month-old by a neighbor's nanny. After learning that the person who blinded her daughter was still working as a child care provider, she established TrustLine with assistance from other parents, child care advocates and the California legislature. Any parent in California can call TrustLine (800-822-8490) to see if a provider (nanny, babysitter, etc.) is registered and has passed a background check and fingerprint screening. If the provider is not listed with TrustLine, the parent may request it as terms for employment. The cost is $90, which may be paid by the provider, split, or paid by the parents. TrustLine's registry provides access to the national FBI records so if a provider has a serious criminal conviction in another state, it will follow them.

Be prepared, however, because it does take time. An FBI clearance takes two to three months while the California checks can take anywhere from four to six weeks or less (two to three weeks if you pay an additional fee for faster service fee).

Since 1995, all subsidized child care providers within the state of California have been required to register with TrustLine. Nanny agencies in California are also required to register the child care providers they place.

According to Cindy Swanson, program manager for the California Child Care Resource & Referral Network (San Francisco), more than 1,000 applications are received each month and 89 percent of them pass. You can also reach TrustLine on the Internet at: www.trustline.org.

Many states are looking to establish similar programs.

Video Surveillance

Establishing a mutually respectful and trusting relationship with your child care provider is important, so if you are considering using video surveillance, you may want to inform your child care provider in advance. But remember, if you feel uncomfortable with your child care provider or sense something isn't quite right, you do not have to prove it with a videotape. You can terminate their employment without video proof.

If you want to explore this option, there are a number of companies that will provide video surveillance of your home so you can monitor what goes on while you're at work. Companies such as The Baby Channel, Babywatch, KinderCam, Nanny Check, Inc., Nanny Watch, A Parent's

View, Seemychild.Com, Watch It, Inc., and Watch Me!, to name just a few, offer a wide variety of options and costs (including installing a small camera in a stuffed animal that can be moved from room to room).

This is one investment parents pray will not pay off.

For more information, look in the yellow pages of the telephone book under "Surveillance and Security Systems" or check out the Internet using "child care surveillance" as a search topic.

Speaking of the World Wide Web

Personal computers and the Internet can be used to access all kinds of valuable information. The World Wide Web, which resides on the Internet, contains many web sites dedicated to the topic of child care.

For those of you who are new to this technology, the best way to tap into this resource is to use a standard web browser such as Netscape Navigator to sample some of the web sites listed below. You can also use any search engine, such as Yahoo! Search or WebCrawler, to locate additional resources by simply entering something like "child care" or "nanny services" in the search form. Your search will probably return hundreds of sites that meet your search criteria, but you can narrow these down by making your criteria more specific, possibly by limiting yourself to a specific state or region.

The following web sites are a small sample of what is available that may help parents find quality child care. Make sure to carefully assess any source you find on the Web. While many of these sites are supported by legitimate organizations that maintain accurate and up-to-date data, some are generated by less reliable, possibly even fly-by-night groups or individuals. The list below is not intended as an endorsement of any of these sites or organizations, but merely a good starting point for parents using the Web to research their child care options.

Parents Place: **http://www.Parentsplace.com/**

A grassroots meeting ground for parents to connect, communicate and celebrate the adventures of child rearing. Also, women's health, child development, pet peeves and so on.

Parenting: **http://www.parentingqa.com/**

Ask the experts about child care and parenting in general. An excellent resource for parents with kids of all ages.

Parent Soup: **http://www.parentsoup.com/**

One of the best web sites available for comprehensive information about parenting issues offers outstanding chat rooms with access to professionals.

Careguide: **http://www.careguide.net**
Another outstanding resource for child care and elder care.

Parents of Children with Disabilities: **http://www.php.com/**
Parents of children with disabilities can connect with others through chat rooms, support groups and events. Also offers resource and book information.

Trish & John's Resource for Parents with Disabilities:
http://ourworld.compuserve.com
Great resource covers books, support groups, organizations, accessible/adaptive parenting products and much more, including links to other web sites for parents with disabilities.

Bizy Moms: **http://www.snowcrest.net/forger/**
The Stay at Home Mom's Guide to Making Money, by Liz Folger Interviews from 29 successful work-at-home moms plus practical tips on how to begin your own home-based business while avoiding scams.

Solo: A Guide for the Single Parent
http://pages.prodigy.com/solo/guide.htm
A quarterly publication. Solo is designed to answer questions about new findings in finance, law, child psychology, custody disputes, coping strategies and success stories, all relating to the single parent.

Parents Without Partners:
http://www.parentsplace.com/readroom/pwp/
Living alone, child issues, widowhood and more.

Parent Time: **http://www.pathfinder.com/parenttime/welcome/**
A definitive Web resource for moms and dads with special information on raising kids ages 0–6 years.

Nap Time Notes: **http://www.ddc.com/napnotes/**
Really cute stories you can read while the kids sleep. You will relate!

National Center for Fathers: **http://www.fathers.com**
Connect with other dads and receive tips and training to develop fathering skills.

Dad Stories: **http://www.dads.com**
Funny essays about fatherhood.

Internet Resources for Special Children: **http://www.irsc.org/**

The emphasis is on *ability* rather than disability. Invaluable to parents, teachers, therapists and others.

Special Needs: **http://www.specialneeds.com/**
Book topics from allergies to . . . you name it.

ADD – What Parents Should Know:
http://www.chadd.org/ doe/doe
A guide to help parents recognize attention deficit disorder and develop an action plan.

National Attention Deficit Disorder Association: **http://www.add.org**
Teens and young adults with/ADD can find lots of information.

Steps and Stages of Bedwetting:
http://www.todaysparent.com/steps.and.stages/
A *Today's Parent* article on causes and treatment of bed-wetting.

Toilet Training: **http://www.parentingme.com.**
Tips and information condensed from the book by Dr. Brenda Hussey-Gardner.

Mothers Who Think: **http://node54.salon1999.com/ mothers/**
Don't let the name throw you. We know all mothers think (although sometimes I doubt myself). Various aspects of motherhood—interviews, short fiction and on-line discussion and personal stories.

Homeworking Business Links: **http://www.homeworkingmom.com**
Ideas, inspiration and support for mothers who choose to work at home.

Adoptive Families of America: **http://www.adoptivefam.org/**
Resources for adoption and parenting. Also, links to other sites.

Postpartum Education for Parents:
http://www.marketmedia.com/pep/
Publications, support and information for postpartum distress, also known as "baby blues."

Moms Online—A Home for Moms in Cyberspace:
http://www.momsonline.com/
Message boards, ask the pros, recipes, moms making a difference, hot tips and more.

Mid-life Mommies: **http://www.cris.com/**

For older moms to share experiences with others, and explore avenues for a healthy pregnancy.

Full-Time Dads: **http://www.slowlane.com/ftd/**
Electronic publication offers news and articles perfect for stay-at-home dads. Published six times a year.

A Father's Journal: **http://top.monad.net**
One man's personal story of fatherhood. A syndicated column by Forrest Seymour.

Dad's in the Kitchen: **http://www.dinersgrapewine.com**
Ever tasted a cow cone? Lots of recipes and advice from Michael Krauss. Well-written (funny) and very practical.

At Home Dad:
http://www.parentsplace.com/readroom/athomedad/index.html
Newsletter aimed at more than 2 million dads who are the primary caregivers for their children. Distributed quarterly ($15/year).

Kids Source On-line: **http://www.kidsource.com/**
Lots of in-depth articles about all kinds of kids; also chat rooms.

Child Lures: **http://www.childlures.com**
Child safety tips, resources, research and statistics aimed at protecting kids from child abuse and abduction.

Sleep Trivia: **http://www.landandsky.com/trivia.html**
Learn more about your children's sleep patterns.

Reading Rainbow: **http://www.pbs.org/ readingrainbow/**
Broadcast schedule, and program descriptions for the PBS program *Reading Rainbow*. Also offers activity suggestions and more.

Mister Rogers Neighborhood: **http://www.pbs.org/rogers**
Who can resist? Play along, sing along and get a personal message from Mr. Rogers himself.

Children's Weight Management Center:
http://www.kidsweight.com/
Help your family work together to create a healthier lifestyle.

Federal Office of Child Support Enforcement:
http://www.acf.dhhs.gov/ACFprograms

Basic facts relating to federal child support laws and their enforcement.

Super Kids: **http://www.superkids.com**

Reviews of children's software titles by parents, kids and teachers. Summary tables identify key attributes to help you select the most appropriate software for your child.

Preemie Resources: **http://home.vicnet.net**

Information about prematurely born babies. Web sites, organizations, financial assistance, books and pamphlets.

Dyslexia: **http://www.medicinenet.com/**

Learn more about this reading difficulty—lots of information, resources and help.

100 Best Companies for Working Mothers:
http://www.women.com/work/best

The title says it all.

Family Relations: **http://www.personal.psu.edu/faculty**

Information about relationships, parenting, siblings, grandparents, family problems and other links.

A Woman's Space: **http://www.womansspace.com**

Movie reviews, recipes, health, nutrition, consumerism.

National Network for Child Care:
http://www.exnet.iastate.edu/Pages/families/nncc/

Choosing quality child care, health and safety information, balancing work and family, e-mail discussion group and more.

Child and Family Canada: **http://www.cfc-efc.ca/**

Sponsored by the Canadian Child Care Federation, this site offers information on child care, parenting, health, play, media influences, nutrition and more. In English and French.

Child Care Action Website:
http://www.freenet.hamilton.onca/~ab608/Profile.html

Discusses the characteristics of a quality child care environment, health fact sheets, suggested reading and more.

NaniNet—Nanny Employment Placement and Referral Connection:
http://www.nannynetwork.com/

Searchable database of in-home child care resources, plus other resources for nannies and families who employ nannies.

National Association for the Education of Young Children:
http://www.naeyc.org/default.htm
Public policy updates, tips for finding an accredited early childhood/child care program and guidelines on developmentally appropriate practices.

Child Care Experts National Network:
http://www.childcare-experts.org/
Designed to help parents and employers access information about child development.

Index

Boldface page numbers indicate main discussion of a topic.

support groups 16, 102
Swanson, Cindy 171

T

telephone interview **31–35**
television shows 1–3
Texas 63
three- to five-year-olds. *See* preschoolers
toddlers 21–22
toilet training 22
TrustLine 171
two-year-olds 22–23

U

Union Bank (Monterey Park, Calif.) 90
unlicensed homes 14

V

vacations 102
video surveillance 171–172
voice mail 30–31

W

walking 101
web sites 172–177
weekend care 53
White, Burton L. 21
women, in workforce 86–87
word of mouth 28, 80–81
World War II 3
World Wide Web 172–177

Y

yellow pages 80
YMCA programs 77